Building Investor-Ready Companies for Public Markets

How to Attract Institutional Investors and Prepare for Market Entry

By Joe Correa

Published by Live Stronger Faster

This book is for educational and informational purposes only. The author and publisher are not engaged in rendering legal, financial, or other professional advice. Readers should consult a qualified professional before making any financial decisions.

First Edition

Table of Contents

The journey toward taking a company public is not merely about reaching a certain revenue number, obtaining legal approvals, or ringing the opening bell of a stock exchange. The true challenge lies in building a company that institutional investors trust, understand, and believe can continue growing for years into the future. Public markets reward companies that are structured, scalable, transparent, and capable of surviving economic cycles while continuing to create shareholder value. This is why some businesses receive massive valuations and overwhelming investor demand, while others struggle to attract serious capital despite having good products or impressive sales growth.

In today's world, capital flows toward companies that can clearly communicate a compelling long-term story backed by strong operational systems, leadership stability, financial discipline, and scalable market opportunities. Institutional investors are not merely buying products or services. They are buying future expectations. They are investing in the belief that a company can continue expanding revenue, protecting margins, increasing market share, and navigating competitive pressures over time. This means that building an investor-ready company requires far more than

Introduction

The journey toward taking a company public is not simply about reaching a certain revenue number, obtaining legal approvals, or ringing the opening bell on a stock exchange. The true challenge lies in building a company that institutional investors trust, understand, and believe can continue growing for years into the future. Public markets reward companies that are structured, scalable, transparent, and capable of surviving economic cycles while continuing to create shareholder value. This is why some businesses receive massive valuations and overwhelming investor demand while others struggle to attract serious capital despite having good products or impressive sales growth.

In today's world, capital flows toward companies that can clearly communicate a compelling long-term story backed by strong operational systems, leadership stability, financial discipline, and scalable market opportunities. Institutional investors are not merely buying products or services. They are buying future expectations. They are investing in the belief that a company can continue expanding revenue, protecting margins, increasing market share, and navigating competitive pressures over time. This means that building an investor-ready company requires far more than entrepreneurship alone. It requires strategic preparation, professionalization, and the transformation of a business into an organization capable of operating under the intense scrutiny of public markets.

Many founders begin their entrepreneurial journey with passion, hustle, creativity, and the willingness to take risks that others avoid. In the early stages, companies often operate informally. Decisions may be centralized around the founder. Financial systems may be simple. Hiring may occur rapidly without fully developed infrastructure. Marketing may depend heavily on personal relationships or founder-driven branding. These methods can help a company survive and even grow during its private stages. However, institutional investors evaluate companies through a completely different lens. Public market investors seek consistency, predictability, governance, operational resilience, and long-term scalability. They want confidence that the company can continue functioning efficiently even if founders step away from daily operations.

This transformation from entrepreneurial startup to investor-ready enterprise is one of the most important evolutions any company can undergo. Businesses that fail to make this transition often struggle during fundraising rounds, experience valuation pressure, or collapse under the weight of public market expectations after listing. On the other hand, companies that prepare strategically for institutional investment create the foundation for sustainable growth, premium valuations, stronger negotiating leverage, and long-term wealth creation opportunities for founders, employees, and shareholders alike.

One of the most misunderstood aspects of investor readiness is the idea that investors only care about revenue growth. While growth is certainly important, sophisticated investors evaluate a much broader set of factors. They analyze market size, competitive positioning, customer acquisition costs, retention metrics, operational efficiency, leadership quality, intellectual property protection, governance structures, scalability, profitability potential, regulatory risks, and overall business durability. A rapidly growing company without systems, controls, or sustainable economics may actually appear more dangerous than attractive to institutional capital providers.

Institutional investors are responsible for managing enormous amounts of capital on behalf of pension funds, insurance companies, university endowments, mutual funds, sovereign wealth funds, and high-net-worth clients. Because of this responsibility, they must evaluate risk carefully. They seek companies capable of generating long-term returns while minimizing the probability of operational instability or catastrophic failure. This means that founders who understand how institutional investors think gain a significant advantage during fundraising, pre-IPO positioning, and public market preparation.

Throughout this book, you will learn that investor readiness is not a single event. It is a process of intentional company development. It involves building financial transparency, operational systems, legal compliance, scalable management structures, strong reporting frameworks, investor communication strategies, and growth models capable of surviving under public scrutiny. The companies that succeed in public markets are rarely the companies with the loudest marketing or the most exciting headlines. Instead, they are often the companies that quietly build strong foundations long before they enter the spotlight.

One of the most powerful concepts in capital markets is that perception drives valuation. Two companies with similar revenue may receive dramatically different valuations depending on how investors perceive future growth, operational quality, risk management, and leadership credibility. Investor confidence can create enormous wealth expansion. Weak investor confidence can destroy valuations almost overnight. This is why public market preparation requires founders to think strategically about branding, communication, governance, investor relations, and long-term positioning. Many entrepreneurs spend years focused exclusively on customers while paying very little attention to investors. However, once a company approaches institutional funding or public market ambitions, investors effectively become another customer segment that must be understood and served strategically. Investors want clarity. They want transparency. They want realistic guidance rather than exaggerated promises. They want leadership teams that understand both opportunities and risks. They want businesses with repeatable systems rather than chaotic growth dependent on founder personality alone.

This shift in thinking is critical because public companies operate under constant evaluation. Analysts review quarterly earnings reports. Institutional investors compare performance metrics against competitors. Financial journalists scrutinize leadership decisions. Regulators monitor disclosures and compliance practices. Shareholders evaluate management execution. Public markets are unforgiving environments where confidence can rise or collapse quickly depending on company performance and communication. Therefore, companies that prepare early for these realities position themselves far more effectively for long-term success.

Investor readiness also extends beyond financial metrics into leadership psychology and organizational culture. Institutional investors place enormous importance on management quality because leadership teams ultimately determine whether strategic plans become reality. Investors want leaders who demonstrate discipline, adaptability, accountability, communication skills, and emotional stability under pressure. Public companies experience volatility, criticism, economic shifts, competitive threats, and operational challenges. Leadership teams that panic, overreact, or communicate poorly can quickly erode investor trust.

This means that founders must evolve personally alongside their businesses. The mindset required to launch a startup is often different from the mindset required to lead a public company. Early-stage entrepreneurship rewards speed, improvisation, and aggressive risk-taking. Public company leadership requires measured decision-making, structured planning, governance discipline, stakeholder communication, and operational consistency. Founders who successfully navigate this transition often become exceptionally wealthy because they learn how to scale not only their businesses, but also themselves.

Another major component of investor readiness is the development of scalable infrastructure. Institutional investors want to see evidence that growth can continue without operational breakdowns. Companies approaching public markets must demonstrate reliable accounting systems, cybersecurity protections, compliance frameworks, internal controls, reporting systems, legal protections, and operational workflows capable of supporting larger transaction volumes and workforce expansion. Investors know that rapid growth without infrastructure often creates instability that eventually damages profitability and reputation.

Technology plays an increasingly important role in this process. Modern investors evaluate how companies use automation, data analytics, artificial intelligence, customer relationship management systems, operational dashboards, and financial reporting technologies to improve efficiency and scalability. Companies that leverage technology effectively often appear more investable because they can scale revenue while controlling operational costs more efficiently than competitors.

Market positioning is another key factor institutional investors evaluate carefully. Investors seek companies operating within industries that possess strong long-term growth potential. They analyze whether the company has competitive advantages that can protect future market share. These advantages may include brand strength, intellectual property, network effects, recurring revenue models, proprietary technology, distribution advantages, customer loyalty, or regulatory barriers that limit competition. In many cases, investors are less concerned with where a company is today than where it could be five or ten years into the future. This is why storytelling becomes such an important skill in public market preparation. Founders must learn how to communicate a believable vision for future growth while supporting that vision with credible execution plans and measurable performance indicators. Great investor communication combines inspiration with discipline. It creates excitement while maintaining realism and trust.

As companies approach IPO preparation, investor relations become increasingly important. Investor relations involve far more than marketing presentations or earnings calls. It is the ongoing process of building credibility and maintaining trust with the investment community. Companies that establish strong investor communication practices early often experience smoother fundraising processes, stronger institutional participation, and more stable shareholder relationships after going public.

This book will help you understand how sophisticated investors evaluate businesses and what separates average companies from truly investor-ready enterprises. You will learn how companies build credibility before public listings, how management teams position themselves strategically, how governance structures influence investor confidence, and how scalable operational systems contribute to premium valuations. You will also explore how market perception, communication strategies, leadership development, and financial discipline combine to influence long-term capital market success.

Importantly, this book is not only for billion-dollar startups or Silicon Valley technology companies. The principles of investor readiness apply across industries and business sizes. Whether a company operates in technology, finance, healthcare, manufacturing, real estate, energy, consumer products, artificial intelligence, education, or services, institutional investors consistently evaluate many of the same foundational characteristics. Companies that learn these principles early gain enormous strategic advantages over competitors that remain reactive and unprepared.

You will also discover that building an investor-ready company creates benefits even if a business never goes public. Companies with strong systems, governance, reporting, scalability, and leadership discipline are often more profitable, more stable, easier to manage, and more attractive to private investors, acquisition buyers, strategic partners, and lenders. In many ways, preparing for institutional investment forces entrepreneurs to build stronger businesses overall.

The road toward becoming an investor-ready company is demanding, but it is also transformational. It pushes founders to think bigger, build smarter systems, improve financial discipline, strengthen leadership capabilities, and position their businesses for long-term sustainability rather than short-term survival. The companies that embrace this evolution often create extraordinary wealth—not only through public listings, but through the long-term value generated by disciplined execution and strategic growth.

As you move through this book, you will gain insight into the psychology of institutional investing, the mechanics of public market preparation, and the structural foundations required to attract serious capital. You will learn how companies position themselves before IPOs, how investor confidence influences valuation expansion, and how founders can strategically prepare for larger equity events and liquidity opportunities.

The public markets have created some of the greatest wealth-building events in modern history. Behind every successful IPO is a company that spent years developing operational maturity, investor credibility, leadership strength, and scalable systems capable of supporting long-term growth. Investor readiness is not about appearances alone. It is about building a business that truly deserves institutional confidence.

This book is designed to help you understand how that transformation happens—and how you can apply these principles to build a stronger company, attract larger pools of capital, and create long-term wealth through disciplined growth and strategic public market preparation.

Chapter 1

Understanding What Institutional Investors Really Want

One of the biggest misconceptions entrepreneurs have about raising institutional capital is the belief that investors are simply looking for exciting ideas, fast growth, or innovative products. While those elements certainly matter, institutional investors operate according to a far more sophisticated framework. They are not only searching for businesses with potential. They are searching for businesses capable of generating reliable, scalable, long-term returns while managing risk effectively over time. Understanding this distinction is one of the most important steps any founder can take when preparing a company for institutional investment or public markets.

Institutional investors control enormous amounts of capital. Pension funds, hedge funds, mutual funds, sovereign wealth funds, insurance companies, private equity firms, venture capital firms, and large family offices collectively manage trillions of dollars globally. These organizations have fiduciary responsibilities to protect and grow the money entrusted to them. Because of this, they evaluate investment opportunities with discipline, structure, and detailed analysis. They cannot afford to make emotional decisions based solely on hype or short-term excitement. Instead, they focus heavily on sustainability, scalability, leadership quality, operational systems, financial controls, market opportunities, and long-term value creation.

Many founders spend years building products without fully understanding how professional investors evaluate businesses. A company may have passionate customers and impressive revenue growth, yet still fail to attract institutional capital if investors perceive operational instability, inconsistent financial reporting, weak management structures, legal exposure, or unclear long-term strategy. Institutional investors are not only evaluating whether a company can grow. They are evaluating whether the company can survive adversity, scale efficiently, compete over time, and continue producing shareholder value under public scrutiny.

One of the first things institutional investors analyze is market opportunity. Investors want to know whether the company operates within a large and expanding market capable of supporting long-term growth. Even an excellent company can struggle to attract capital if the total addressable market is too small. Investors seek industries where significant expansion remains possible. They want businesses positioned within trends that may continue for years or even decades. These trends may involve artificial intelligence, healthcare innovation, financial technology, renewable energy, cybersecurity, digital media, logistics, cloud computing, real estate technology, biotechnology, automation, or consumer behavioral shifts.

A company operating in a rapidly expanding market immediately gains a strategic advantage because investors recognize the possibility of future scale. However, being in a large market alone is not enough. Investors also evaluate competitive positioning. They want to understand what differentiates the company from competitors and whether that advantage can be maintained over time. This competitive advantage may involve proprietary technology, intellectual property, network effects, branding, customer loyalty, distribution systems, operational efficiency, recurring revenue models, or unique market access.

Companies without defensible advantages often face valuation pressure because investors fear future competition may reduce profitability. Institutional investors constantly ask themselves difficult questions. What prevents competitors from copying this business model? How strong is customer retention? Does the company have pricing power? How scalable are operations? Can margins improve as the company grows? How dependent is the business on economic cycles? How exposed is the company to regulation or technological disruption? These questions form the foundation of institutional investment analysis.

Leadership quality represents another critical factor investors evaluate intensely. Many institutional investors believe management quality is one of the most important variables influencing long-term company success. Investors know that markets change, competition evolves, and unexpected challenges emerge constantly. Strong leadership teams can adapt strategically while weak leadership teams often collapse under pressure. This is why investors spend significant time analyzing founders, executives, and management culture before making investment decisions.

Investors evaluate whether leadership teams possess vision, discipline, operational expertise, emotional stability, communication skills, and strategic thinking abilities. They look for founders capable of attracting talent, building systems, solving problems, managing crises, and executing long-term growth plans. Institutional investors also pay attention to leadership maturity. Founders who exaggerate projections, avoid accountability, or communicate inconsistently often create concern because public markets demand transparency and credibility. In many cases, investors are more comfortable investing in an average business with an exceptional management team than in an exceptional product led by inexperienced or unstable leadership. Public companies operate under constant pressure from analysts, shareholders, regulators, competitors, and media scrutiny. Investors want confidence that management teams can navigate these pressures professionally while continuing to grow the business strategically.

Financial transparency is another major area institutional investors prioritize. Sophisticated investors expect accurate financial reporting, organized accounting systems, internal controls, and reliable forecasting processes. Companies approaching institutional funding or IPO preparation must demonstrate the ability to produce consistent financial statements and operational metrics. Investors want visibility into revenue growth, profit margins, customer acquisition costs, retention rates, debt obligations, cash flow, and scalability trends.

Many early-stage businesses operate with incomplete financial systems. Founders may rely on simple bookkeeping, inconsistent reporting, or reactive decision-making. While this may work temporarily during startup phases, institutional investors view poor financial controls as a major red flag. Weak accounting systems create uncertainty, and uncertainty increases perceived risk. Investors are far more likely to fund companies that demonstrate financial discipline and operational organization.

Predictability is one of the most valuable characteristics investors seek. Public markets reward companies capable of delivering consistent performance over time. Predictable businesses allow investors to model future earnings, estimate risk more accurately, and assign higher valuations with greater confidence. This is why recurring revenue models, subscription businesses, long-term contracts, and stable customer retention often receive premium valuations in capital markets.

Institutional investors also care deeply about scalability. A company may be profitable today, but investors want to know whether growth can continue without causing operational collapse. They analyze whether the company's infrastructure can support expansion into larger markets, additional geographies, or increased customer volume. Businesses dependent entirely on founder involvement often struggle to appear scalable because investors worry operations cannot function independently.

Scalable companies typically possess standardized systems, repeatable processes, automation capabilities, strong middle management, operational documentation, and technology infrastructure capable of supporting growth. Investors want to see that revenue can increase faster than costs over time. Companies capable of improving operational efficiency while expanding revenue often achieve significantly higher valuations because investors anticipate stronger future profitability.

Another factor institutional investors examine closely is customer concentration risk. Companies overly dependent on one customer, one supplier, or one revenue source may appear unstable. Investors prefer diversified revenue streams because diversification reduces vulnerability to unexpected disruptions. If one customer accounts for fifty percent of company revenue, investors may worry about catastrophic downside risk if that relationship deteriorates.

Similarly, investors analyze industry concentration, geographic concentration, and operational dependency risks. Businesses with diversified customer bases, multiple growth channels, and broad market exposure often appear more resilient and attractive to institutional capital providers.

Corporate governance becomes increasingly important as companies approach public market readiness. Governance refers to the systems, policies, structures, and oversight mechanisms guiding company decision-making and accountability. Institutional investors pay close attention to board composition, executive compensation, shareholder protections, compliance practices, and ethical leadership standards.

Public markets depend heavily on investor trust. Companies with weak governance structures often face skepticism because poor oversight increases the likelihood of fraud, operational failures, regulatory issues, or leadership abuse. Strong governance signals professionalism, accountability, and maturity. Investors want assurance that leadership decisions align with shareholder interests and long-term value creation rather than short-term personal gain.

Communication skills also play a major role in investor confidence. Institutional investors expect management teams to communicate clearly, honestly, and strategically. Public companies must regularly explain performance results, growth strategies, risks, and market conditions. Investors dislike surprises. Companies that fail to communicate effectively often experience stock volatility, reduced credibility, and valuation declines.

This is why investor relations become such an essential component of public market preparation. Investor relations involve the ongoing management of communication between the company and the investment community. Strong investor communication builds trust, strengthens credibility, and helps stabilize shareholder relationships during periods of volatility or uncertainty.

Institutional investors also evaluate long-term vision. They want to know whether the company has a believable strategy for future expansion and competitive positioning. Investors understand that businesses evolve over time. They seek leadership teams capable of adapting intelligently while maintaining strategic focus. A company without a clear long-term roadmap may appear directionless, even if short-term performance remains strong.

Importantly, institutional investors think in probabilities rather than guarantees. They understand that no company is perfect and no investment is risk-free. Their goal is to identify businesses where the probability of long-term success outweighs the probability of failure. Every factor they evaluate—leadership quality, financial discipline, scalability, market opportunity, governance, customer diversification, operational systems, and strategic clarity—contributes to their perception of risk versus reward.

Founders who understand this mindset gain a major advantage because they begin building companies through the eyes of investors rather than solely through the eyes of operators. They recognize that investor readiness is not simply about achieving revenue milestones. It is about building trust, reducing perceived risk, and creating confidence in the company's long-term future.

Many of the world's most successful public companies spent years developing investor-ready characteristics before entering public markets. They invested heavily in systems, governance, reporting, leadership recruitment, operational infrastructure, and strategic positioning long before filing for IPOs. These preparations allowed them to attract institutional capital more effectively and often contributed to stronger public market debuts.

Another important reality founders must understand is that institutional investors often evaluate qualitative factors as heavily as quantitative metrics. Numbers matter tremendously, but perception, trust, credibility, leadership behavior, and market confidence also influence valuations significantly. Two companies with similar financial performance may receive dramatically different valuations depending on how investors perceive management quality, future growth potential, operational maturity, and strategic positioning.

This is why investor readiness involves both operational excellence and narrative development. Founders must build strong businesses while also learning how to communicate compelling long-term visions supported by credible execution. Investors invest in future possibilities, not just current performance. The ability to articulate how the company may evolve over time becomes incredibly valuable during fundraising and IPO preparation.

Public market investing is ultimately built on confidence. Investors place capital into businesses they believe can continue creating value over many years. Every operational improvement, leadership upgrade, financial control, governance enhancement, and strategic initiative contributes to building that confidence.

As companies progress toward institutional funding or public listings, founders must begin thinking differently. They must shift from survival-focused entrepreneurship toward scalable organizational leadership. This evolution requires discipline, strategic planning, operational maturity, and a deep understanding of what sophisticated investors truly value.

The companies that master this transition often unlock extraordinary opportunities. They gain access to larger pools of capital, stronger partnerships, premium valuations, acquisition leverage, and long-term wealth creation pathways unavailable to less prepared competitors. Investor readiness is not merely about raising money. It is about transforming a company into an enterprise capable of thriving within the demanding environment of institutional capital and public markets.

The Founder Who Learned to Think Like Wall Street

When Daniel Reyes started his software company from a small apartment in Miami, he never imagined institutional investors would one day compete to own shares in his business. In the beginning, the company was little more than an idea supported by relentless effort, long nights, and financial desperation. Daniel had no prestigious MBA, no venture capital connections, and no wealthy family members funding his dream. He simply believed there had to be a better way for small businesses to automate customer communication without hiring massive support teams.

The first version of the platform barely functioned. Daniel spent months teaching himself coding, customer acquisition, digital marketing, and product design simultaneously. During the day he worked consulting jobs to pay rent. At night he built software features while responding personally to customer emails. For nearly two years the business generated little revenue, and many people quietly assumed the company would fail like most startups.

Yet Daniel possessed something many entrepreneurs lacked. He listened carefully to customers and adapted quickly. Small business owners consistently complained about losing leads because they could not respond to inquiries fast enough. Daniel refined the software repeatedly until it became highly effective at automating text messages, email follow-ups, and appointment scheduling. Slowly, customers began referring other customers.

Within three years the company reached several million dollars in annual recurring revenue. Daniel felt unstoppable. Revenue was growing quickly, customers seemed happy, and social media attention surrounding the business increased dramatically. He assumed institutional investors would immediately recognize the opportunity and rush to invest.

However, Daniel's first meetings with venture capital firms were disastrous.

One investor questioned why customer churn remained elevated. Another asked about cybersecurity protocols. Another demanded audited financial statements Daniel did not have. Several investors expressed concern that too much of the company depended on Daniel personally. Others questioned whether the company could scale internationally. One investor politely told Daniel that while the product was impressive, the company itself was not "institutional grade."

Daniel left those meetings frustrated and confused. He believed growth alone would attract capital. Instead, investors seemed focused on risks, systems, infrastructure, governance, and long-term scalability. For the first time, Daniel realized there was a major difference between building a fast-growing startup and building an investor-ready company.

That realization changed everything.

Rather than becoming defensive, Daniel decided to study institutional investing obsessively. He began reading annual reports, studying IPO filings, listening to earnings calls, and analyzing how successful public companies communicated with investors. He realized that sophisticated investors evaluated businesses through frameworks completely different from the mindset of early-stage entrepreneurs.

Institutional investors cared deeply about predictability. They wanted recurring revenue stability, retention improvements, operational scalability, compliance systems, executive leadership depth, and reliable forecasting models. They wanted confidence that the business could survive market downturns and continue producing long-term shareholder value.

Daniel realized his company still operated like a startup built around his personality rather than a scalable enterprise capable of supporting institutional ownership.

Over the next three years, he transformed the business systematically.

First, he recruited experienced executives. He hired a CFO with public company experience, a chief technology officer specializing in cybersecurity infrastructure, and an operations executive who had scaled software companies internationally. Daniel initially resisted surrendering control, but he soon realized strong leadership teams increased investor confidence dramatically.

Next, the company invested heavily in operational systems. Financial reporting became standardized. Internal controls were implemented. Customer support processes became automated and measurable. Legal compliance improved. Data analytics dashboards tracked customer behavior, churn, retention, and profitability with precision.

Daniel also focused heavily on reducing customer concentration risk. Previously, a handful of large clients represented too much revenue. The company diversified aggressively into multiple industries and customer segments, reducing vulnerability significantly.

Most importantly, Daniel learned how to communicate strategically. He stopped exaggerating projections and began presenting realistic growth models supported by operational data. Investors noticed the difference immediately. Meetings shifted from skepticism toward genuine interest.

By the sixth year, the company looked entirely different. Revenue surpassed one hundred million dollars annually. Churn declined dramatically. Profit margins improved. International expansion accelerated. Most importantly, institutional investors now viewed the business as scalable, disciplined, and credible.

Major investment firms began competing to participate in late-stage funding rounds. Analysts described the company as one of the fastest-growing investor-ready software platforms in its sector. Daniel finally understood that investors were not simply buying growth. They were buying confidence in the future.

The company eventually prepared for an IPO.

During the roadshow, Daniel met with institutional investors across New York, Boston, Chicago, San Francisco, and London. This time, the conversations felt entirely different from the painful meetings years earlier. Investors asked sophisticated questions about expansion strategy, market penetration, operating leverage, and long-term margin potential. Daniel answered calmly with data, clarity, and strategic discipline.

When the company finally listed publicly, demand exceeded expectations. Institutional orders flooded in. The valuation surpassed several billion dollars. Financial news networks praised the company's operational maturity, recurring revenue strength, and disciplined leadership team.

On the morning of the IPO, Daniel stood quietly inside the stock exchange before the opening bell ceremony. Cameras flashed around him while employees celebrated nearby. Yet Daniel's mind drifted back to those humiliating early investor meetings when he first realized his company was not ready.

He now understood the most important lesson of his entrepreneurial journey.

Building an investor-ready company was not about convincing Wall Street to believe in him. It was about transforming the business into something that genuinely deserved institutional confidence.

That transformation changed not only the company's valuation, but Daniel himself. He no longer thought like a struggling founder focused only on survival. He thought like a long-term capital allocator, strategic leader, and public market executive.

Years later, Daniel often mentored younger entrepreneurs preparing for fundraising. Many assumed investors cared primarily about hype, rapid growth, or media attention. Daniel would smile and explain that sophisticated investors cared about something far more valuable.

They cared about trust.

Trust in leadership.

Trust in systems.

Trust in financial discipline.

Trust in long-term scalability.

Trust that the company could survive adversity and continue creating value year after year.

Daniel learned that institutional capital flows toward businesses capable of earning that trust consistently. And once a company earns that confidence, the opportunities for growth, valuation expansion, and wealth creation become almost limitless.

Chapter 2

Creating Scalable Systems That Institutional Investors Trust

One of the defining differences between a small private business and an investor-ready company is the existence of scalable operational systems. Institutional investors are not simply investing in products, ideas, or short-term revenue growth. They are investing in systems capable of producing sustainable growth repeatedly and predictably over long periods of time. A company may generate impressive sales today, but if its operations depend entirely on founder involvement, inconsistent workflows, or fragile infrastructure, sophisticated investors will often view the business as high-risk regardless of current profitability.

Scalability is one of the most important characteristics institutional investors seek because scalable companies possess the potential to increase revenue dramatically without experiencing proportional increases in expenses, operational chaos, or management breakdowns. Public market investors want businesses capable of expanding efficiently while maintaining customer satisfaction, operational consistency, financial discipline, and profit potential. Companies that achieve this balance often receive premium valuations because investors believe future growth can occur in a sustainable manner.

Many entrepreneurs initially build businesses through improvisation. In the early stages, founders often perform multiple roles simultaneously. They handle sales, marketing, operations, customer support, hiring, accounting, product development, and strategic planning themselves. Decisions happen quickly and informally. Processes may exist only inside the founder's mind. While this flexibility can help startups survive during their earliest phases, it eventually becomes a liability if the company intends to attract institutional investment or pursue public market ambitions.

Institutional investors evaluate whether a business can continue operating effectively without excessive dependence on any single individual. If a company cannot function efficiently when the founder takes a vacation for one week, investors may question whether the organization is truly scalable. Businesses overly dependent on founder involvement create operational risk because growth eventually becomes constrained by the founder's personal capacity. Sophisticated investors prefer companies where systems, teams, and processes drive growth rather than founder exhaustion alone. One of the first areas investors analyze is operational consistency. They want to know whether the company can deliver predictable outcomes repeatedly. Consistency creates confidence because it reduces uncertainty. Investors examine whether products are delivered reliably, customer experiences remain stable, financial reporting is accurate, and operational performance can be measured objectively over time. Companies with inconsistent operations often experience unpredictable financial performance, customer dissatisfaction, employee turnover, and scalability challenges.

Documented systems play a major role in creating operational consistency. Investor-ready companies typically develop standard operating procedures for critical business functions. These procedures create repeatable workflows that employees can follow regardless of leadership changes or rapid growth. Standardization reduces operational chaos and improves scalability because the company no longer relies exclusively on memory, improvisation, or informal communication.

For example, an investor-ready company may develop detailed procedures for customer onboarding, sales qualification, marketing campaigns, compliance reviews, product fulfillment, quality control, hiring, training, cybersecurity, accounting, and reporting. These systems allow the business to scale more efficiently because new employees can integrate into structured processes rather than depending entirely on direct founder supervision. Technology infrastructure also becomes increasingly important as companies scale toward institutional readiness. Investors want to see businesses leveraging technology strategically to improve efficiency, automate repetitive tasks, analyze operational data, and support future growth. Modern investors understand that companies capable of integrating technology effectively often scale faster and more profitably than competitors relying on outdated manual systems.

Automation allows businesses to reduce operational bottlenecks while increasing productivity. Customer relationship management platforms, enterprise resource planning systems, data analytics dashboards, automated billing systems, cloud infrastructure, artificial intelligence tools, workflow automation software, and cybersecurity protections all contribute to operational maturity. Companies that invest in scalable technology infrastructure often appear more sophisticated and future-oriented to institutional investors.

Data visibility is another critical component of scalable systems. Institutional investors expect management teams to understand their businesses through measurable metrics rather than intuition alone. Investor-ready companies track operational key performance indicators carefully and use data-driven decision-making processes to improve efficiency and profitability. Depending on the industry, these metrics may include customer acquisition cost, lifetime customer value, gross margins, churn rates, employee productivity, operational turnaround times, recurring revenue retention, inventory turnover, software engagement metrics, market penetration rates, and profitability trends. Investors want leadership teams capable of analyzing these metrics intelligently and making strategic adjustments based on real operational insights.

One reason public markets reward data-driven companies is because measurable systems improve forecasting reliability. Investors value predictability because predictable companies are easier to analyze and model financially. Companies capable of forecasting revenue, margins, customer growth, and operational performance accurately often earn stronger investor confidence. Reliable forecasting suggests operational discipline, strong leadership visibility, and effective internal systems.

Scalability also requires effective organizational structure. As businesses grow, founders must transition from controlling every decision personally toward building teams capable of operating independently. Institutional investors evaluate whether management structures can support larger operational scale without creating inefficiency or confusion.

This often involves creating clear reporting structures, departmental leadership roles, accountability frameworks, performance measurement systems, and communication channels. Companies lacking organizational clarity frequently experience internal dysfunction as they grow. Employees may duplicate efforts, priorities may conflict, and decision-making may become chaotic. Investors recognize these risks and often penalize companies that appear operationally disorganized.

Recruiting talent becomes increasingly important during this stage of growth. Institutional investors understand that scaling companies require strong teams, not just visionary founders. Investor-ready companies attract experienced executives, operational leaders, financial professionals, legal advisors, technology experts, and departmental managers capable of supporting long-term expansion.

One major sign of operational maturity is when leadership depth exists beyond the founder alone. Investors gain confidence when businesses possess capable management teams with specialized expertise and succession potential. Companies where every major decision still flows through one individual often appear fragile because growth becomes constrained by centralized control.

Cybersecurity and risk management have also become central concerns for institutional investors. As companies scale digitally and store increasing amounts of customer data, operational risk expands significantly. Investors evaluate whether businesses possess adequate cybersecurity protections, data privacy practices, backup systems, regulatory compliance frameworks, and operational continuity plans.

A rapidly growing company without proper risk management infrastructure may appear dangerous regardless of revenue growth. Investors know that operational disruptions, data breaches, regulatory violations, or compliance failures can destroy shareholder value quickly. Therefore, institutional capital increasingly flows toward companies demonstrating operational resilience and proactive risk management practices.

Another important element investors analyze is operational leverage. Operational leverage refers to a company's ability to increase revenue faster than operating expenses over time. Businesses with strong operational leverage become increasingly profitable as they scale because fixed costs remain relatively stable while revenue expands.

Software companies often illustrate this concept clearly. Once software infrastructure is developed, additional customers may generate high-margin recurring revenue without significantly increasing operational expenses. Investors value these business models highly because scalable economics create the potential for substantial future profitability.

However, operational leverage exists across many industries. Manufacturing companies may improve production efficiency through automation. Service businesses may standardize processes to improve employee productivity. Financial companies may scale through digital platforms. E-commerce businesses may optimize fulfillment systems to support higher sales volume efficiently. Institutional investors constantly analyze whether businesses possess scalable economic structures capable of producing stronger margins over time.

Culture also influences scalability more than many founders realize. Investor-ready companies often develop cultures emphasizing accountability, communication, adaptability, and operational discipline. Strong cultures improve execution because employees understand expectations clearly and align around long-term company objectives.

Companies with toxic internal cultures frequently struggle during scaling phases. Rapid growth can magnify communication problems, leadership weaknesses, employee dissatisfaction, and operational confusion. Institutional investors increasingly evaluate employee retention, leadership culture, diversity practices, and organizational health because these factors influence long-term operational sustainability.

One challenge many founders face is balancing innovation with operational discipline. Early-stage startups often thrive through creativity, speed, and experimentation. However, institutional investors seek evidence that growth can occur within structured operational frameworks. Investor-ready companies learn how to preserve innovation while implementing systems capable of supporting sustainable scale.

This balance becomes particularly important during public market preparation. Public companies must meet regulatory reporting requirements, maintain financial transparency, manage investor expectations, and operate under continuous scrutiny. Companies lacking scalable operational systems often struggle after IPOs because public market demands expose internal weaknesses rapidly.

Many failed IPOs share similar patterns. Revenue growth initially attracts investor excitement, but operational inefficiencies, poor controls, inconsistent execution, or weak leadership eventually damage investor confidence. Public markets are unforgiving environments where operational problems become highly visible. This is why companies preparing for institutional investment must strengthen systems long before entering public markets. Another critical factor institutional investors evaluate is adaptability. Scalable companies must not only handle growth, but also respond effectively to changing market conditions. Economic downturns, technological shifts, competitive threats, supply chain disruptions, regulatory changes, and customer behavior changes all require operational flexibility.

Companies with rigid or outdated systems may struggle to adapt quickly. Investor-ready companies build infrastructure that supports both stability and flexibility. Leadership teams monitor market trends continuously and implement operational improvements proactively rather than reactively.

Importantly, scalable systems do not eliminate entrepreneurial vision. Instead, they allow visionary ideas to expand beyond the limitations of founder capacity. Many founders resist implementing structure because they fear bureaucracy or reduced creativity. However, institutional investors understand that systems create scalability, and scalability creates enterprise value.

Without systems, businesses remain dependent on constant heroic effort. With systems, businesses become capable of compounding growth efficiently over time.

As companies mature, institutional investors increasingly reward operational excellence. Businesses with scalable systems often attract larger funding rounds, stronger strategic partnerships, premium acquisition interest, and higher public market valuations. Investors trust organizations capable of producing consistent execution because consistency reduces perceived risk.

Ultimately, scalable systems transform companies from fragile entrepreneurial operations into durable enterprises capable of supporting institutional ownership and long-term public market participation. Investors are not simply looking for companies that can grow quickly. They are looking for companies capable of growing intelligently, sustainably, and predictably over time.

The founders who understand this distinction begin building infrastructure long before institutional investors demand it. They recognize that operational maturity is not a burden—it is a competitive advantage. Strong systems create efficiency, confidence, resilience, and scalability. These characteristics form the foundation of investor-ready companies capable of attracting serious capital and generating long-term wealth creation opportunities.

The Company That Nearly Collapsed From Its Own Growth

When Samantha Lee launched her logistics software company, she believed speed was everything. She admired aggressive startup founders who preached rapid scaling, nonstop growth, and dominating markets before competitors could react. Samantha built her company with relentless intensity. She recruited customers aggressively, pushed employees to work long hours, and celebrated every revenue milestone as proof that the business was succeeding.

At first, the strategy appeared brilliant.

The company's software helped shipping companies optimize delivery routes and reduce transportation costs. Demand exploded as fuel prices increased and supply chain inefficiencies became more expensive worldwide. Within three years, Samantha's company grew from a small startup into one of the fastest-growing logistics platforms in the country.

Revenue tripled repeatedly. Investors praised the growth numbers. Industry blogs featured Samantha as a rising technology entrepreneur. New customers signed contracts almost daily. Samantha became obsessed with expansion.

But behind the scenes, the company was beginning to crack.

Customer onboarding lacked consistency because every sales

representative promised different implementation timelines. Support tickets piled up because customer service systems were disorganized. Software bugs increased because developers rushed updates without proper testing procedures. Accounting reports often contained errors because financial systems had not scaled with company growth.

Employees constantly worked in crisis mode.

Most decisions still depended on Samantha personally. Department leaders waited for her approval before moving forward on important initiatives. She answered customer complaints herself late at night while simultaneously negotiating contracts, reviewing payroll, approving marketing campaigns, and handling investor meetings.

The company looked successful from the outside, but internally it operated like controlled chaos.

Samantha ignored the warning signs because revenue continued growing. She assumed problems could be solved later. Growth became the company's only focus.

Then the largest client in company history signed a multi-million-dollar contract.

At first, Samantha celebrated aggressively. She believed the deal validated everything she had built. Investors congratulated her. Employees cheered during company meetings. Revenue projections soared.

However, onboarding the new client exposed every weakness inside the organization. The implementation team lacked standardized deployment procedures. Communication failures delayed integration timelines. Customer support representatives received conflicting instructions from management. Software infrastructure struggled to handle increased transaction volume. Developers worked around the clock attempting emergency fixes.

The client became increasingly frustrated.

Meetings turned tense. Deadlines slipped repeatedly. Customer complaints escalated. Internally, employees blamed one another for failures because responsibilities were unclear.

Then disaster struck.

During a major shipping cycle, the platform experienced a severe system outage that disrupted delivery operations for several large customers simultaneously. The outage lasted nearly fourteen hours. Some customers lost millions of dollars in delayed logistics coordination.

The backlash was immediate.

Customers threatened lawsuits. Social media criticism spread rapidly. Industry publications questioned whether the company had scaled irresponsibly. Several major clients canceled contracts within weeks. Most devastating of all, institutional investors preparing a large funding round suddenly withdrew interest.

One investor delivered the harshest feedback Samantha had ever received.

"You built growth," he told her quietly during a private meeting. "But you didn't build infrastructure."

Those words haunted her.

For the first time, Samantha realized revenue growth alone did not create an investor-ready company. The business lacked operational maturity. Systems had not evolved alongside growth. The company depended too heavily on improvisation and founder control rather than scalable operational discipline.

Samantha faced a painful decision. She could continue pretending everything was fine while hoping growth recovered, or she could rebuild the company properly.

She chose reconstruction.

The next eighteen months became the hardest period of her career.

The company hired experienced operational executives from larger technology firms. Standard operating procedures were created across every department. Financial systems were upgraded completely. Customer onboarding became standardized. Cybersecurity infrastructure improved dramatically. Software testing protocols became mandatory before deployments.

Samantha also transformed her leadership style.

Instead of controlling every decision personally, she focused on building leadership teams capable of operating independently. Department accountability structures became clear. Performance metrics were tracked carefully. Data dashboards monitored customer satisfaction, software stability, implementation timelines, and operational efficiency continuously.

At first, growth slowed significantly. Some employees resisted the increased structure. Samantha occasionally worried the company was becoming too corporate and losing its entrepreneurial culture.

But gradually, stability emerged.

Customer retention improved dramatically. System outages decreased. Employee turnover fell. Financial reporting became reliable. Operational forecasting improved. Most importantly, the company regained credibility.

Institutional investors eventually returned. This time, investor conversations felt very different. Instead of focusing solely on growth rates, investors praised the company's operational maturity, leadership discipline, infrastructure improvements, and scalable systems.

One investor told Samantha something she never forgot.

"Fast growth attracts attention," he said. "Scalable systems attract institutional capital."

Years later, Samantha often spoke publicly about the experience. Many young founders expected her to emphasize aggressive scaling strategies. Instead, she warned entrepreneurs about the dangers of scaling faster than operational infrastructure could support.

She explained that investors ultimately trust systems more than hype.

Systems create consistency.

Systems create predictability.

Systems reduce risk.

Systems allow businesses to grow sustainably without collapsing under pressure.

Samantha eventually took the company public successfully. By then, the organization operated with the discipline, reporting standards, operational controls, and leadership depth expected of a public enterprise.

Looking back, Samantha realized the company's near-collapse had been one of the greatest lessons of her life.

Growth alone did not build enterprise value.

Scalable systems did.

And once those systems existed, the business became far more valuable, resilient, investable, and capable of long-term wealth creation than it had ever been during its chaotic early growth years.

Chapter 3

Leadership, Governance, and Building Public Market Credibility

As companies move closer toward institutional investment and public market readiness, leadership quality and governance structures become increasingly important. Many founders initially believe investors care primarily about revenue growth, product innovation, or market size. While those elements remain critical, sophisticated institutional investors also place enormous weight on the people leading the organization and the systems governing decision-making. Public markets depend heavily on trust, and trust is built through credible leadership, accountability, transparency, and disciplined governance practices.

The transition from a private entrepreneurial company to a public-market-ready organization requires founders to evolve significantly. In the early stages of a startup, decision-making is often fast, informal, and centralized around the founder. Entrepreneurs may rely heavily on instinct, speed, and improvisation. These qualities can help companies survive during uncertain startup phases. However, public companies operate under entirely different expectations. Institutional investors expect leadership teams capable of managing complexity, communicating clearly, operating transparently, and making disciplined long-term decisions under constant scrutiny.

Public markets are unforgiving environments. Investors analyze quarterly performance, analysts evaluate forecasts, journalists investigate executive behavior, regulators monitor disclosures, and shareholders scrutinize management decisions continuously. Because of this, investors place substantial importance on whether leadership teams possess the maturity and stability required to navigate these pressures successfully.

One of the first things institutional investors evaluate is leadership credibility. Credibility refers to the degree of confidence investors have in management's honesty, competence, and execution ability. Investors want to believe that leadership teams understand their businesses deeply, communicate realistically, and can execute strategic plans effectively over long periods of time.

Leadership credibility is built slowly but can be destroyed quickly. Founders who exaggerate projections, overpromise results, hide operational weaknesses, or communicate inconsistently often lose investor trust rapidly. Once credibility weakens, restoring confidence becomes extremely difficult.

Public markets frequently punish companies not only for poor performance, but also for surprises that damage investor confidence.

This is why transparency becomes such a critical component of investor-ready leadership. Institutional investors understand that every company faces risks, operational challenges, and market uncertainty. Investors do not necessarily expect perfection. However, they do expect leadership teams to communicate openly about risks, explain problems honestly, and present realistic strategies for addressing challenges. Transparency reduces uncertainty, and reduced uncertainty increases investor confidence.

Another essential leadership quality investors evaluate is strategic thinking. Public companies must balance short-term operational execution with long-term growth planning. Investors seek leadership teams capable of allocating capital intelligently, adapting to changing markets, identifying future opportunities, and maintaining strategic focus during periods of volatility.

Short-term thinking often destroys long-term shareholder value. Companies that prioritize temporary stock price increases over sustainable operational strength frequently encounter serious problems later. Institutional investors prefer leadership teams capable of making disciplined decisions that support long-term enterprise value creation rather than reactive decisions driven by short-term market pressure.

Capital allocation represents one of the most important responsibilities public company leadership teams face. Institutional investors evaluate how management deploys company resources, including acquisitions, hiring, research and development spending, technology investments, debt management, share buybacks, and expansion initiatives. Strong capital allocators often create enormous long-term shareholder wealth because they deploy resources efficiently toward high-return opportunities.

Weak capital allocation decisions, however, can destroy enterprise value rapidly. Companies that overspend recklessly, pursue poorly structured acquisitions, accumulate excessive debt, or invest heavily in low-return projects often experience declining investor confidence. This is why institutional investors pay close attention to leadership judgment, financial discipline, and strategic prioritization.

Another important factor investors analyze is leadership depth. In early-stage startups, founders often control nearly every major function. While this may work temporarily, institutional investors typically prefer organizations with experienced executive teams capable of operating independently. Businesses dependent entirely on one charismatic founder may appear risky because leadership concentration creates operational vulnerability.

Investor-ready companies usually develop strong management teams with specialized expertise across finance, operations, legal compliance, technology, marketing, and strategy. Leadership depth reassures investors because it suggests the company can continue functioning effectively even during leadership transitions or periods of founder absence.

Succession planning also becomes increasingly important as companies mature. Institutional investors often ask difficult questions about leadership continuity. What happens if the founder retires unexpectedly? Is there a pipeline of capable executives prepared to assume greater responsibility? Are operational systems dependent on a single personality? Investors seek organizations capable of surviving leadership changes without major operational disruption.

Governance structures help reinforce leadership accountability and organizational stability. Corporate governance refers to the systems, policies, oversight mechanisms, and decision-making frameworks guiding company operations and protecting shareholder interests. Strong governance practices create confidence because they reduce the probability of fraud, operational abuse, regulatory violations, or reckless leadership behavior.

One major component of governance is board structure. Institutional investors pay close attention to board composition, independence, expertise, and oversight quality. Effective boards provide strategic guidance, monitor executive performance, oversee risk management, and protect shareholder interests. Public market investors generally prefer boards containing experienced independent directors capable of challenging management decisions objectively when necessary.

Companies with weak or overly founder-controlled boards often raise governance concerns because investors worry insufficient oversight may lead to poor decision-making or excessive executive power concentration. Strong boards contribute significantly to public market credibility because they signal operational maturity and accountability.

Audit practices also play a major role in governance evaluation. Institutional investors expect investor-ready companies to maintain rigorous financial reporting standards and independent auditing processes. Reliable financial reporting strengthens investor trust because it improves visibility into company performance and reduces concerns regarding accounting irregularities or financial manipulation.

Internal controls become especially important as companies scale. Internal controls include the systems and procedures designed to ensure financial accuracy, operational accountability, regulatory compliance, and fraud prevention. Weak controls increase operational risk significantly, particularly for companies preparing for public listings where regulatory scrutiny intensifies substantially.

Regulatory compliance itself represents another critical governance area. Public companies must comply with extensive disclosure requirements, securities regulations, reporting standards, and corporate governance obligations. Institutional investors prefer companies that proactively build compliance infrastructure before public listing rather than reacting defensively after regulatory issues emerge.

Ethical leadership also influences investor confidence more than many founders realize. Institutional investors increasingly evaluate environmental, social, and governance factors when making investment decisions. Companies associated with unethical behavior, toxic workplace cultures, discrimination, corruption, or leadership misconduct often experience reputational damage that negatively impacts valuation and investor participation. Public markets operate heavily on perception. A single ethical controversy involving leadership behavior can erase billions of dollars in market value within days. Because of this, investor-ready companies often invest heavily in compliance programs, ethics training, employee protections, cybersecurity protocols, diversity initiatives, and governance frameworks designed to reduce reputational risk.

Communication skills become critically important once companies enter public market environments. Leadership teams must communicate effectively with shareholders, analysts, employees, regulators, media outlets, and institutional investors simultaneously. Poor communication can create confusion, uncertainty, and stock volatility even when operational performance remains strong.

Investor-ready executives learn how to communicate strategically while maintaining transparency and credibility. They provide realistic guidance rather than exaggerated promises. They explain risks clearly. They remain calm during difficult periods. They avoid emotional reactions to short-term market volatility. Consistent communication builds investor trust over time.

Emotional discipline itself is one of the most underrated leadership characteristics institutional investors value. Public companies face constant pressure, criticism, competition, and unpredictable market conditions. Investors prefer leaders capable of making rational long-term decisions during stressful periods rather than reacting impulsively to temporary challenges.

Many founders struggle with this transition because startup culture often rewards aggressive confidence and relentless optimism. Public markets, however, reward measured leadership, operational discipline, and strategic consistency. Investor-ready founders learn how to balance ambition with realism and vision with accountability.

Another important aspect of leadership credibility involves alignment with shareholders. Institutional investors evaluate executive compensation structures, insider ownership levels, and incentive systems carefully. Investors prefer leadership teams whose financial incentives align with long-term shareholder value creation rather than short-term stock price manipulation.

Founders who maintain meaningful ownership stakes often appear more aligned with shareholders because their personal wealth remains connected to long-term company performance.

At the same time, investors also seek compensation structures encouraging sustainable growth rather than excessive risk-taking. Institutional investors additionally evaluate company culture because culture influences execution quality, employee retention, innovation, and operational resilience. Strong cultures often create competitive advantages because employees align around shared values, accountability standards, and long-term objectives.

Companies with toxic internal cultures frequently experience operational instability, leadership turnover, reduced innovation, reputational damage, and declining morale. Public markets eventually notice these problems because poor culture often manifests through declining execution quality and weakened financial performance over time.

Leadership visibility also matters significantly in public markets. CEOs and executive teams effectively become representatives of the company brand itself. Investors evaluate how leaders conduct interviews, handle earnings calls, respond to crises, and communicate strategy publicly. Strong leadership presence can strengthen investor confidence dramatically, while poor leadership communication can create uncertainty and skepticism.

Importantly, public market leadership is not about perfection. Investors understand that every company encounters setbacks and challenges. What matters most is how leadership responds during difficult periods. Transparent communication, disciplined decision-making, operational accountability, and strategic adaptability often strengthen investor trust even during temporary adversity.

The most respected public companies often share similar leadership characteristics. They communicate consistently. They prioritize long-term strategy over short-term hype. They maintain strong governance systems. They develop leadership depth. They build cultures focused on accountability and execution. They understand that credibility compounds over time just like financial performance.

For founders preparing companies for institutional investment or IPO pathways, leadership development becomes just as important as operational growth. Building investor-ready credibility requires personal evolution alongside company expansion. Founders must transition from startup operators into strategic enterprise leaders capable of managing complexity, accountability, and public market expectations.

Ultimately, institutional investors are not only investing in businesses. They are investing in leadership teams they trust to manage capital responsibly, allocate resources intelligently, navigate adversity effectively, and create long-term shareholder value consistently. Strong governance and credible leadership reduce perceived risk, strengthen investor confidence, support premium valuations, and create the foundation for sustainable long-term public market success. Companies that prioritize these elements early often gain substantial advantages as they scale toward institutional ownership and broader capital market participation.

The CEO Who Almost Lost Wall Street's Trust

When Michael Carter founded his renewable energy company, investors loved him immediately. He was charismatic, confident, visionary, and persuasive. During interviews, he spoke passionately about transforming the global energy industry and building one of the largest clean technology companies in the world. Employees admired his intensity. Venture capital firms praised his ambition. Journalists described him as one of the brightest entrepreneurs of his generation.

The company itself grew rapidly.

Its solar energy storage technology gained attention from commercial real estate developers and industrial manufacturers seeking lower energy costs. Revenue expanded quickly. Strategic partnerships increased. New investors entered funding rounds aggressively, hoping the company would become one of the next major public market success stories. Michael embraced the attention completely.

He appeared constantly on podcasts, business television programs, and industry conferences. Investors loved hearing him discuss future expansion plans, international growth opportunities, and billion-dollar market potential. The company's valuation increased dramatically with every funding round.

Internally, however, problems were beginning to emerge.

Senior executives quietly complained that Michael frequently made impulsive decisions without consulting leadership teams. Financial projections provided to investors often appeared overly optimistic compared to internal operational realities. Product development timelines were rushed publicly even when engineers warned they were unrealistic.

Several executives worried the company was prioritizing appearances over operational discipline.

But few challenged Michael directly because he remained the face of the company and controlled most strategic decisions personally.

Eventually, the company prepared for an IPO.

Institutional investors initially showed strong interest. The renewable energy sector remained attractive, and the company's growth story generated excitement across financial markets. Analysts described the IPO as one of the most anticipated offerings of the year.

Then problems surfaced during due diligence.

Institutional investors reviewing company operations discovered inconsistencies between public projections and internal forecasts. Several operational delays had not been fully disclosed externally. Employee turnover among senior management appeared unusually high. Internal controls lacked maturity compared to other IPO candidates.

One major investment fund privately informed the underwriting banks that leadership credibility had become a concern.

Word spread quickly throughout institutional circles.

Investors began questioning whether Michael prioritized publicity more than operational transparency. Analysts became skeptical regarding long-term forecasts. Financial journalists started investigating executive turnover and internal governance concerns.

Suddenly, the IPO no longer looked guaranteed.

Michael reacted emotionally. During internal meetings, he blamed executives, market conditions, and skeptical investors rather than acknowledging leadership weaknesses. Publicly, he continued projecting confidence, but institutional investors increasingly viewed his communication style as defensive and overly promotional.

The company's valuation expectations dropped sharply.

For the first time in his career, Michael realized charisma alone could not sustain investor confidence indefinitely. Public markets required something deeper—credibility.

The board intervened aggressively.

Independent directors demanded governance reforms, stronger internal controls, more realistic financial guidance, and leadership restructuring. Michael initially resisted. He viewed the criticism as unfair attacks against his vision.

But eventually, one conversation changed his perspective completely.

An experienced board member named Richard Hale requested a private dinner meeting.

Richard had previously served as CEO of a major public technology company and understood Wall Street deeply. During dinner, he listened quietly while Michael defended himself passionately. Finally, Richard interrupted him.

"You built excitement," Richard said calmly. "But public markets don't reward excitement forever. They reward trust."

Michael remained silent.

Richard continued.

"Investors can tolerate setbacks. They can tolerate temporary losses. They can tolerate economic cycles. What they cannot tolerate is uncertainty about leadership credibility."

That sentence stayed with Michael for weeks.

Gradually, he began reevaluating how he led the company.

Instead of focusing primarily on media attention and aggressive projections, Michael shifted toward operational discipline and transparent communication. Financial guidance became more conservative and data-driven. Leadership meetings became collaborative rather than centralized around his personal decisions.

The company strengthened internal controls significantly. Governance policies improved. Independent board oversight expanded. Executive turnover stabilized. Most importantly, Michael learned how to communicate honestly about both opportunities and risks.

Institutional investors slowly regained confidence.

The company delayed its IPO temporarily while restructuring internally. Although painful initially, the delay ultimately strengthened the organization substantially. Operational systems matured. Forecasting accuracy improved. Investor communication became disciplined and credible.

Two years later, the company returned to public markets.

This time, institutional investors responded very differently.

During the IPO roadshow, investors noticed Michael's transformation immediately. He no longer exaggerated projections or dismissed operational risks casually. He communicated strategically, transparently, and calmly. Analysts respected the company's disciplined reporting. Investors trusted leadership credibility far more than before.

The IPO succeeded successfully, raising billions in capital.

After the public listing, one journalist asked Michael during an interview what the biggest lesson of his entrepreneurial journey had been.

Michael smiled thoughtfully before answering.

"I used to think investors were buying vision," he said. "But eventually I learned they're really buying trust in leadership execution."

Over the following decade, the company became one of the most respected renewable energy businesses in public markets. Analysts consistently praised management credibility, governance quality, operational discipline, and long-term strategic execution.

Michael himself changed profoundly as a leader.

He no longer chased headlines obsessively. He focused instead on building systems, strengthening culture, improving transparency, and allocating capital carefully. Investor trust became something he protected relentlessly.

Years later, Michael often mentored younger founders preparing for IPOs. Many believed strong branding, aggressive growth projections, or media popularity would automatically attract institutional investors.

Michael would quietly explain that public markets ultimately evaluate something much deeper.

They evaluate whether leadership deserves trust during both success and adversity.

Because in capital markets, credibility is not merely a public relations asset.

It is one of the most valuable forms of capital a company can possess.

Chapter 4

Financial Transparency, Reporting Discipline, and Investor Confidence

One of the most important foundations of institutional investment and public market readiness is financial transparency. Investors allocate capital based on trust, and trust depends heavily on the accuracy, consistency, and reliability of financial information. Public markets function efficiently only when investors believe companies are presenting truthful representations of their operational performance, financial condition, growth potential, and risk exposure. Without financial transparency, investor confidence deteriorates quickly, valuations decline, and access to capital becomes increasingly difficult.

Many entrepreneurs underestimate how important financial reporting becomes as companies scale toward institutional funding or IPO preparation. In early-stage businesses, founders often prioritize product development, customer acquisition, sales growth, and operational survival while treating financial systems as secondary concerns. Informal bookkeeping, inconsistent reporting, limited forecasting, and reactive financial management may temporarily support small private operations. However, institutional investors evaluate businesses very differently. They expect companies seeking serious capital to demonstrate financial discipline, reporting accuracy, operational visibility, and forecasting reliability.

Sophisticated investors understand that financial statements tell a story about the health and maturity of a business. Revenue growth alone rarely provides a complete picture. Investors analyze profit margins, operating efficiency, recurring revenue stability, debt levels, cash flow management, customer acquisition costs, retention metrics, capital expenditures, operational leverage, and long-term sustainability. Reliable financial reporting allows investors to evaluate whether growth is profitable, scalable, and durable.

One reason financial transparency matters so much is because institutional investors think in terms of risk management. Investors understand that every company faces uncertainty. Their goal is not to eliminate all risk, but to evaluate risk accurately. When financial reporting lacks clarity or consistency, uncertainty increases dramatically. Higher uncertainty causes investors to apply lower valuations, demand stricter investment terms, or avoid investing altogether.

This is why companies with strong financial controls often command significantly higher valuations than companies with weak reporting systems, even when revenue levels appear similar. Investors pay premiums for visibility and predictability because these qualities reduce perceived risk.

Public companies operate under particularly intense financial scrutiny. Quarterly earnings reports, annual filings, analyst coverage, regulatory disclosures, and shareholder expectations create environments where financial accuracy becomes essential. Companies that fail to meet reporting standards or surprise investors negatively often experience sharp declines in market value and investor trust.

The foundation of financial transparency begins with accounting discipline. Investor-ready companies develop accurate bookkeeping systems, standardized accounting procedures, independent auditing practices, and internal financial controls long before entering public markets. These systems create consistency, improve decision-making, and reduce the probability of reporting errors or financial manipulation.

Many institutional investors strongly prefer audited financial statements because audits increase confidence in reporting accuracy. Independent auditors review company financial records, internal controls, accounting methodologies, and operational processes to ensure compliance with accepted standards. While audits cannot guarantee perfection, they significantly improve investor confidence by introducing external oversight and accountability.

Accrual accounting also becomes increasingly important as companies mature. Small businesses often operate primarily on cash-based accounting systems that track money entering and leaving accounts. However, institutional investors typically expect accrual accounting because it provides more accurate visibility into company performance by matching revenues and expenses within the periods they are actually earned or incurred.

Investor-ready companies must also demonstrate strong cash flow management. Revenue growth means little if a company consistently burns excessive cash without sustainable economics. Investors analyze operating cash flow carefully because cash generation reflects operational health more accurately than revenue growth alone in many cases.

Companies with poor cash flow management may appear fragile even when revenue grows rapidly. Businesses that require constant outside funding to survive often face investor skepticism unless they operate within sectors where long-term scalability clearly justifies temporary losses. Public market investors increasingly favor companies capable of balancing growth with improving operational efficiency and financial sustainability.

Forecasting ability represents another major factor institutional investors evaluate closely. Investor-ready companies must demonstrate the ability to project future financial performance with reasonable accuracy. Forecasting involves estimating future revenue, expenses, margins, hiring needs, capital requirements, and operational trends based on measurable data and strategic planning.

Reliable forecasting signals operational maturity because it demonstrates management visibility into company performance drivers. Companies consistently missing projections or changing guidance dramatically often lose investor confidence because unpredictable financial performance increases uncertainty.

Importantly, investors generally tolerate occasional operational challenges or temporary setbacks more easily than poor communication or unreliable forecasting. Public markets understand that businesses operate in dynamic environments. However, leadership credibility suffers significantly when management repeatedly overpromises and underdelivers.

This is why conservative guidance often strengthens investor confidence more effectively than aggressive projections.

Experienced executives understand that credibility compounds over time. Companies that consistently meet or exceed expectations typically develop stronger long-term investor relationships than companies constantly chasing unrealistic growth narratives.

Financial transparency also extends beyond income statements and balance sheets into operational metrics. Institutional investors increasingly expect detailed reporting regarding customer behavior, retention, recurring revenue trends, profitability segmentation, geographic performance, and operational efficiency indicators.

Software companies, for example, may report annual recurring revenue, net revenue retention, customer acquisition costs, lifetime customer value, and churn metrics. Consumer companies may report same-store sales growth, inventory turnover, customer engagement trends, or geographic expansion performance. Industrial companies may disclose production efficiency, supply chain stability, or operational utilization metrics.

Operational transparency helps investors understand how businesses actually function internally. Detailed metrics improve investor confidence because they provide visibility into performance drivers beyond headline revenue numbers.

Another critical aspect of financial discipline involves capital structure management. Institutional investors evaluate debt levels, liquidity reserves, equity dilution, financing strategies, and balance sheet strength carefully. Companies overly dependent on debt financing may appear vulnerable during economic downturns or rising interest rate environments.

Investor-ready companies typically maintain thoughtful balance sheet strategies that support growth while preserving operational flexibility. Strong liquidity positions reassure investors because they reduce concerns regarding short-term financial distress or emergency fundraising needs.

Working capital management also influences investor perception significantly. Businesses must manage receivables, payables, inventory, operational expenses, and cash conversion cycles efficiently. Poor working capital management may indicate operational inefficiency or financial instability, even when revenue appears healthy.

Public market investors additionally pay close attention to margin trends. Revenue growth attracts attention, but margin expansion often drives long-term valuation increases because improving margins suggest operational leverage and scalability. Companies capable of growing revenue while improving efficiency often receive premium market valuations due to anticipated future profitability potential. Financial transparency becomes especially important during periods of market volatility or operational adversity. Companies inevitably face challenges such as economic slowdowns, competitive pressure, supply chain disruptions, regulatory changes, or temporary performance declines. During these periods, investor confidence depends heavily on management communication and reporting discipline.

Companies that communicate clearly during difficult periods often preserve investor trust even when short-term performance weakens. On the other hand, companies that obscure problems, delay disclosures, or provide misleading guidance frequently experience severe reputational damage once issues become public.

The collapse of investor confidence can occur extremely quickly in public markets. History contains numerous examples of companies whose valuations collapsed after accounting irregularities, misleading financial disclosures, or governance failures emerged. These situations reinforce why institutional investors prioritize transparency and financial discipline so heavily.

Internal controls play a major role in protecting reporting integrity. Internal controls include systems designed to ensure financial accuracy, operational accountability, fraud prevention, regulatory compliance, and data security. Investor-ready companies implement controls proactively because strong oversight reduces operational risk substantially.

Segregation of duties, approval hierarchies, audit procedures, cybersecurity protections, compliance reviews, and documentation standards all contribute to stronger financial governance. Institutional investors prefer companies where financial reporting processes appear structured, disciplined, and professionally managed.

Another increasingly important area involves regulatory compliance and disclosure obligations. Public companies must comply with strict reporting standards and securities regulations. Failure to meet these obligations can result in legal liability, regulatory penalties, shareholder lawsuits, and reputational damage.

Investor-ready companies begin preparing for these requirements long before public listing. They invest in legal counsel, compliance infrastructure, reporting systems, and governance processes designed to support future public market obligations efficiently.

Financial discipline also influences company culture. Organizations emphasizing accountability, data-driven decision-making, and operational visibility often execute more effectively than businesses operating reactively without measurable performance standards. Employees within disciplined organizations understand expectations clearly and align around measurable objectives.

Importantly, financial transparency is not simply about satisfying investors. Accurate reporting improves strategic decision-making internally as well. Leadership teams make better operational decisions when they possess reliable visibility into profitability drivers, cost structures, customer trends, and operational performance.

Many entrepreneurs initially resist financial discipline because they associate structure with bureaucracy. However, institutional investors recognize that disciplined financial systems create stability, scalability, and operational intelligence. Strong reporting infrastructure allows businesses to scale intelligently rather than blindly.

As companies approach institutional funding or IPO readiness, financial transparency becomes one of the strongest indicators of operational maturity. Investors understand that businesses with reliable reporting systems, forecasting discipline, strong controls, and transparent communication practices are generally better equipped to navigate public market pressures successfully. Ultimately, investor confidence depends heavily on trust in the numbers. Public markets reward companies capable of producing consistent, accurate, transparent financial reporting because transparency reduces uncertainty and strengthens credibility.

Companies that prioritize financial discipline early gain enormous strategic advantages. They attract stronger investors, negotiate from positions of credibility, access larger pools of capital, and position themselves for sustainable long-term growth within increasingly competitive capital markets.

The Startup That Learned the Hard Way About Financial Discipline

When Olivia Bennett launched her healthcare technology company, she focused on one thing above everything else—growth. Her platform helped clinics automate patient scheduling, insurance verification, and appointment reminders. Customers loved the product because it reduced administrative costs significantly while improving operational efficiency.

The company grew rapidly.

Within four years, revenue expanded from a few thousand dollars annually to nearly fifty million. Venture capital investors praised Olivia constantly. Healthcare conferences invited her to speak regularly. Technology blogs described the company as one of the fastest-growing digital healthcare platforms in the country.

Olivia believed everything was going perfectly.

Internally, however, financial systems remained surprisingly weak.

The accounting department consisted of only a few employees struggling to keep up with company expansion. Financial forecasting was inconsistent. Revenue recognition practices varied across contracts. Expense tracking lacked discipline. Operational reporting systems remained fragmented between departments.

Whenever executives raised concerns about improving financial controls, Olivia pushed the discussions aside.

"We'll fix all that later," she often said. "Right now we need to dominate the market."

Growth became the company's obsession.

Eventually, institutional investors began encouraging Olivia to prepare for an IPO. The company's sector remained highly attractive, and public market conditions appeared favorable. Investment banks approached aggressively, promising strong valuations if the company listed publicly soon. Excitement spread throughout the organization.

Employees anticipated life-changing wealth from stock options. Investors imagined massive returns. Olivia herself began envisioning the company becoming a billion-dollar public enterprise.

Then the underwriting due diligence process began.

At first, Olivia assumed the process would be routine. Instead, institutional analysts uncovered multiple financial reporting inconsistencies almost immediately. Revenue recognition methods differed between customer contracts. Deferred revenue calculations lacked standardization. Expense categorization varied between departments.

Worse still, forecasting accuracy appeared unreliable.

Internal operational data frequently conflicted with externally presented growth projections. Financial models lacked supporting documentation. Some customer retention metrics had been calculated inconsistently over multiple reporting periods.

The problems were not fraudulent, but they revealed something deeply concerning to institutional investors.

The company lacked financial discipline.

Investor confidence weakened quickly.

Investment bankers delayed the IPO timeline while auditors conducted deeper reviews. Analysts began questioning whether the company's operational infrastructure was mature enough for public markets. Institutional investors worried that rapid growth had outpaced financial controls.

Olivia became frustrated and defensive initially.

She argued that the business remained fundamentally strong and customers still loved the product. But during one difficult meeting, an experienced institutional investor explained the problem directly.

"Your company may be growing," he told her calmly, "but public investors need confidence that the numbers are reliable."

That sentence changed everything.

For the first time, Olivia realized institutional investors viewed financial reporting as more than administrative paperwork. Investors saw financial transparency as evidence of operational maturity, leadership discipline, and organizational credibility.

The company postponed its IPO plans. At first, the delay felt humiliating. Media speculation intensified. Competitors criticized the company quietly. Employees worried about the future.

But Olivia made a critical decision.

Instead of rushing toward public markets unprepared, she committed fully to rebuilding the company's financial infrastructure properly.

The transformation was massive.

The company hired an experienced CFO from a public healthcare technology firm. Accounting systems were rebuilt entirely. Independent auditors reviewed operational reporting practices. Revenue recognition standards became standardized. Forecasting processes improved dramatically.

Internal controls expanded across every department.

Operational metrics became measurable and transparent. Financial dashboards gave leadership teams real-time visibility into profitability, expenses, retention, and cash flow.

Budgeting discipline improved. Investor communication became far more conservative and data-driven.

Initially, the changes felt uncomfortable.

Departments accustomed to operating informally resisted increased accountability. Managers disliked stricter reporting standards. Olivia herself struggled occasionally with slower, more disciplined decision-making processes.

But gradually, the organization became stronger.

Forecasting accuracy improved significantly. Cash flow management stabilized. Profit margins increased because operational inefficiencies became visible through better reporting systems. Most importantly, investor confidence slowly returned.

Institutional investors noticed the transformation.

One analyst commented privately that the company now looked "institutional grade" rather than simply "high growth."

Two years later, the company relaunched its IPO process.

This time, investor meetings felt completely different.

Analysts praised reporting transparency. Institutional investors appreciated management discipline. Auditors expressed confidence in internal controls. Financial forecasts appeared credible and measurable rather than overly promotional.

The IPO succeeded successfully, and the company entered public markets with strong investor demand. Years later, Olivia often reflected on the painful experience. She realized her biggest early mistake had been assuming growth alone created enterprise value. In reality, institutional investors valued something equally important—financial trust.

Public markets depended on confidence in reporting accuracy, forecasting discipline, and operational visibility. Without those foundations, even fast-growing businesses appeared risky.

Olivia eventually became known as one of the most disciplined CEOs in the healthcare technology sector. Analysts respected the company's transparency, conservative guidance, and operational consistency.

Ironically, the temporary IPO delay that once felt devastating ultimately became one of the company's greatest advantages.

The rebuilding process forced the organization to mature operationally before entering public markets.

And because of that discipline, the company survived market downturns, industry volatility, and economic uncertainty far more successfully than many competitors that rushed toward public listings without building strong financial foundations first. Olivia later summarized the lesson during an interview with a young entrepreneur.

"Revenue growth may attract investors initially," she said. "But financial transparency is what keeps investor trust over the long term." And in public markets, long-term trust often becomes one of the most valuable assets a company can possess.

Chapter 5

Building a Powerful Investor Narrative and Market Positioning Strategy

One of the most underestimated elements of attracting institutional capital and preparing for public markets is the power of narrative. Many entrepreneurs assume investors make decisions based entirely on spreadsheets, financial ratios, and technical metrics. While financial performance is critically important, institutional investing is also deeply influenced by perception, confidence, and strategic storytelling. Public markets ultimately invest in future expectations, and those expectations are shaped heavily by the narrative surrounding a company.

An investor narrative is the clear, compelling, and believable story a company tells about its mission, market opportunity, competitive advantages, growth potential, and long-term strategy. It explains not only what the company does today, but also why the company may become significantly more valuable in the future. Strong investor narratives create excitement while maintaining credibility. Weak narratives create confusion, skepticism, or indifference. The companies that attract premium valuations often communicate a vision larger than their current financial performance alone.

Institutional investors are constantly searching for businesses capable of dominating large markets, reshaping industries, creating scalable advantages, and generating long-term shareholder value. A strong narrative helps investors understand how a company plans to achieve those outcomes.

Importantly, effective investor narratives are not based on exaggeration or unrealistic hype. Sophisticated investors quickly recognize unsupported claims and promotional language lacking operational substance. Strong narratives combine ambition with evidence. They connect measurable performance data with a believable long-term vision. The goal is not merely to impress investors emotionally, but to help them understand why the company deserves long-term confidence and capital support.

Every successful public company develops some form of strategic market narrative. Technology companies may position themselves as industry disruptors transforming outdated systems. Healthcare companies may emphasize innovation improving patient outcomes and reducing costs. Financial technology businesses may present themselves as democratizing financial access. Consumer brands may focus on loyalty, lifestyle positioning, and global scalability. Industrial companies may highlight operational efficiency, infrastructure modernization, or sustainability trends.

Institutional investors evaluate how clearly companies define their identity within the market. Businesses with vague positioning often struggle to attract investor attention because investors cannot easily understand their competitive advantages or future growth pathways. Clear positioning simplifies investor understanding and strengthens market differentiation.

One of the first components of a strong investor narrative involves defining the problem the company solves. Investors want to understand why the business exists and why customers need its products or services. Companies addressing major inefficiencies, large unmet needs, or rapidly expanding market problems often attract stronger investor interest because their growth potential appears more significant.

The size of the market opportunity also plays a central role in narrative development. Institutional investors generally prefer companies operating within large addressable markets because larger markets support greater long-term expansion potential. Investors often ask whether the company can realistically become a billion-dollar enterprise or even larger over time.

This is why investor-ready companies frequently communicate market opportunity using measurable industry data, demographic trends, technological shifts, consumer behavior changes, or economic transformations. Strong market positioning demonstrates that the company operates within broader long-term trends rather than isolated short-term opportunities.

Competitive differentiation forms another essential component of investor storytelling. Investors constantly evaluate whether competitors can replicate the company's advantages. Strong narratives explain clearly why the company possesses defensible strengths that support long-term market leadership.

These advantages may involve proprietary technology, operational efficiency, intellectual property, network effects, distribution systems, recurring revenue structures, branding strength, regulatory barriers, customer loyalty, or economies of scale. The stronger and more durable the competitive advantages appear, the more attractive the company becomes to institutional investors.

Scalability must also be integrated into the investor narrative. Institutional investors seek companies capable of expanding revenue substantially without proportional increases in operational complexity or expenses. Companies that demonstrate scalable business models often receive premium valuations because investors anticipate stronger future profitability and operational leverage. Recurring revenue models, subscription businesses, software platforms, marketplace ecosystems, and highly automated operations frequently attract strong investor enthusiasm because scalability appears more predictable and sustainable within these structures.

Leadership credibility strongly influences how investors perceive company narratives. Even compelling visions lose effectiveness if investors lack confidence in management execution ability. Investors evaluate whether leadership teams possess the operational discipline, strategic intelligence, communication skills, and industry expertise required to execute long-term growth plans successfully.

This is why investor narratives must align closely with operational reality. Leadership teams that communicate realistic goals supported by measurable progress gradually build strong investor trust. On the other hand, companies promoting unrealistic projections without operational support often damage credibility permanently once expectations fail to materialize.

Timing also matters significantly in market positioning. Institutional investors constantly analyze macroeconomic conditions, industry cycles, technological shifts, and capital market trends. Companies that align their narratives with broader market momentum often attract stronger investor participation.

For example, businesses positioned around artificial intelligence, cybersecurity, renewable energy, digital infrastructure, automation, biotechnology, or financial technology may receive heightened investor interest during periods when those sectors experience strong capital inflows. However, companies must still demonstrate operational substance beyond simply aligning with popular themes.

Investor-ready companies learn how to balance long-term vision with near-term execution. Public markets generally reward companies capable of demonstrating both strategic ambition and operational consistency simultaneously. Investors want to believe the company has enormous future potential while also maintaining confidence that management can execute reliably quarter after quarter.

One major mistake many founders make is attempting to position their companies as everything to everyone. Broad, unfocused narratives often confuse investors because they fail to communicate a clear strategic identity. Strong investor narratives simplify complexity by emphasizing the company's core strengths, market opportunity, and long-term objectives clearly. Consistency becomes extremely important in this process. Investor confidence strengthens when leadership teams communicate consistent messages across earnings calls, investor presentations, interviews, annual reports, and public communications. Inconsistent messaging creates uncertainty, and uncertainty weakens valuation support.

Public market investors also evaluate how companies compare against industry peers. Relative positioning influences valuation significantly because investors often benchmark companies against similar businesses operating within the same sectors. Investor-ready companies understand how they fit within broader market categories and strategically communicate why they deserve premium positioning relative to competitors.

Metrics and storytelling must work together effectively. Financial data without narrative may appear uninspiring. Narrative without supporting metrics appears speculative. Strong investor communication integrates operational performance with strategic vision seamlessly.

For example, a software company may not simply report

revenue growth. It may explain how customer retention improvements demonstrate increasing platform value, how automation reduces operating costs, and how international expansion supports long-term scalability. The narrative transforms raw numbers into a coherent story about future enterprise value creation.

Another important aspect of market positioning involves investor psychology. Institutional investors are influenced not only by fundamentals, but also by confidence, momentum, expectations, and market sentiment. Companies that successfully build strong reputations often attract additional investor interest simply because market confidence itself becomes self-reinforcing.

This phenomenon explains why some companies maintain premium valuations despite temporary setbacks. Investors continue believing in the long-term narrative because management credibility, strategic positioning, and market leadership remain strong. On the other hand, companies lacking strong narratives often experience severe valuation pressure even during minor operational disappointments.

Branding also contributes heavily to investor perception. Public companies increasingly operate as both businesses and public brands simultaneously. Investors evaluate how customers, employees, media outlets, analysts, and industry participants perceive the company overall. Strong branding can improve customer acquisition, attract talent, strengthen partnerships, and reinforce market leadership perceptions. Investor-ready companies understand that perception influences access to capital significantly. Companies perceived as innovative, disciplined, scalable, and strategically positioned often attract institutional capital more easily than companies viewed as operationally weak or strategically unclear.

Another key factor involves long-term vision articulation. Investors want to understand where the company may be five, ten, or even twenty years into the future. Leadership teams capable of explaining believable long-term strategic pathways often generate stronger institutional confidence.

This vision may involve geographic expansion, product diversification, operational automation, acquisitions, technological leadership, ecosystem development, or industry transformation. The stronger the future vision appears—and the more credible management execution becomes—the greater the potential investor enthusiasm.

Importantly, investor narratives evolve over time. Early-stage companies may focus heavily on disruption and market penetration. More mature companies may emphasize profitability, scalability, operational efficiency, and capital allocation discipline. Public companies must continuously refine their narratives as markets, industries, and competitive conditions evolve. Investor relations teams play a major role in managing this process. Effective investor communication strengthens shareholder relationships, improves analyst understanding, and supports valuation stability during periods of volatility or uncertainty.

Companies that fail to manage narratives proactively often allow external perceptions to shape market sentiment instead. Negative media coverage, analyst skepticism, operational surprises, or leadership communication failures can weaken investor confidence rapidly if companies lack strong strategic positioning.

Ultimately, investor narratives shape how institutional capital perceives future opportunity and risk. Strong narratives increase confidence, attract attention, support premium valuations, and create long-term shareholder engagement. Weak narratives create confusion, uncertainty, and valuation pressure.

The most successful public companies understand that financial performance and storytelling are not separate forces.

They work together continuously. Operational execution supports credibility, while narrative helps investors understand why that execution matters within a larger strategic context.

Founders preparing companies for institutional investment must therefore learn how to communicate not only what their businesses are today, but what they may become tomorrow. Public markets invest heavily in future expectations, and companies capable of shaping those expectations credibly often unlock extraordinary wealth creation opportunities over time.

The Founder Who Learned How to Tell the Future

When Ethan Morgan launched his cybersecurity company, he believed the product alone would guarantee success. The software helped businesses detect digital threats using artificial intelligence before attacks could spread across internal networks. The technology worked extremely well, and early customers praised the platform's speed and effectiveness.

Ethan assumed investors would immediately recognize the opportunity.

But the first several years proved disappointing.

Although the company generated steady revenue growth, institutional investors showed limited enthusiasm. Venture capital firms passed repeatedly. Investment bankers seemed polite but unexcited. Analysts described the company as "interesting" but not transformational.

Ethan grew frustrated.

From his perspective, the product clearly solved major problems within cybersecurity. Businesses faced increasing digital threats worldwide, and demand for protection continued growing rapidly. Yet competitors with weaker technology often received far higher valuations and larger funding rounds.

One evening after another disappointing investor meeting in New York, Ethan sat quietly in a hotel lobby reviewing notes from the presentation. An older investor named David Rosen approached him unexpectedly.

David had attended the meeting but barely spoken during the discussion.

"You built a good company," David said calmly as he sat down nearby.

Ethan nodded politely but remained visibly disappointed.

"Then why does nobody seem interested?" he asked.

David smiled slightly.

"Because you're describing software," he replied. "Not a future."

Those words confused Ethan initially.

David continued.

"Investors don't only buy products. They buy narratives about how the world is changing and who will dominate that future."

The conversation lasted nearly two hours.

David explained that Ethan focused too heavily on technical features, product specifications, and operational details while failing to communicate the broader strategic opportunity. Investors did not simply want cybersecurity software. They wanted to understand how cybersecurity itself was evolving globally and why Ethan's company could become a major market leader within that transformation.

For the first time, Ethan realized he had been communicating entirely from an engineer's perspective rather than an institutional investor's perspective.

Over the next several months, Ethan completely reworked the company's positioning strategy.

Instead of describing the business as a software provider, he positioned the company as a future infrastructure platform for automated digital defense systems. Rather than focusing only on current customers, he explained how increasing global cyber threats would force nearly every major business and government institution to adopt predictive AI security systems over the next decade.

The company's narrative shifted from selling software toward protecting the future digital economy itself.

Importantly, Ethan did not exaggerate financial projections or create unrealistic hype. Instead, he connected measurable operational performance with broader industry transformation trends. He demonstrated rising cyberattack frequency, increasing regulatory requirements, growing enterprise security spending, and the limitations of traditional cybersecurity approaches.

Suddenly, investor reactions changed dramatically.

Meetings became more engaging. Institutional investors asked deeper strategic questions. Analysts began viewing the company as part of a massive long-term industry shift rather than simply another software provider.

One investment fund described the company as "positioned at the center of the future cybersecurity infrastructure market."

Valuations increased rapidly.

The business itself had not changed significantly during those months. The technology remained largely the same. Revenue growth remained steady rather than explosive.

What changed was investor perception. Ethan learned how to help investors see not only what the company currently produced, but what role it could play within the future global economy.

As the company scaled, Ethan refined the narrative continuously. Quarterly reports emphasized both operational execution and long-term strategic positioning. Leadership communication remained consistent. Investor presentations aligned closely with measurable performance data.

Institutional confidence grew steadily.

Eventually, major investment banks approached the company regarding IPO preparation. This time, analysts described the business as one of the most strategically positioned cybersecurity firms entering public markets.

During the IPO roadshow, Ethan traveled across New York, Boston, San Francisco, Chicago, and London meeting institutional investors. Many conversations focused less on current revenue and more on the company's future role within global cybersecurity infrastructure.

Ethan now understood something he had missed for years.

Public markets invest heavily in future expectations.

The IPO succeeded beyond expectations.

After the public listing, financial media praised the company's strategic positioning and long-term market vision. Investors viewed the company not merely as a cybersecurity vendor, but as a major participant in the future evolution of digital infrastructure security.

Years later, Ethan often mentored younger founders struggling to attract institutional capital. Many believed better products alone guaranteed investor enthusiasm.

Ethan would explain that while strong products matter enormously, investors also need help understanding why the company matters within a larger future context.

He often summarized the lesson simply.

"A business creates value today," he would say. "But a narrative helps investors imagine how much value the company may create tomorrow."

And in public markets, future expectations often become one of the most powerful forces driving long-term wealth creation.

Chapter 6

Attracting Institutional Capital Before the IPO

One of the most important stages in building a public-market-ready company occurs long before the initial public offering itself. Institutional relationships, investor confidence, operational credibility, and market positioning are often established years before a company officially enters public markets. Businesses that successfully attract institutional capital during private growth stages frequently position themselves for smoother IPO processes, stronger valuations, larger investor participation, and greater long-term stability after listing publicly.

Institutional capital serves as more than simply a funding source. Sophisticated investors often bring strategic guidance, market credibility, operational discipline, industry relationships, and signaling power that can accelerate company development substantially. When respected institutional investors support a company privately, public markets frequently interpret that support as validation of the business model, leadership quality, and long-term growth potential. However, attracting institutional capital is highly competitive. Thousands of businesses seek funding every year, but only a small percentage secure meaningful institutional backing. Investors evaluate opportunities selectively because they manage large pools of capital under significant performance pressure. Understanding how institutional investors think—and what they expect from companies before public listing—is therefore essential for founders preparing businesses for long-term capital market success.

Institutional investors generally invest according to specific mandates, strategies, risk profiles, and return expectations. Venture capital firms may focus heavily on high-growth opportunities with disruptive potential. Private equity firms may prioritize operational improvement and profitability expansion. Growth equity investors may seek companies with proven scalability preparing for larger capital events. Hedge funds may analyze future public market positioning. Sovereign wealth funds and pension funds often seek long-term stability and durable market leadership.

Because institutional investors vary significantly, companies must understand which investors align best with their growth stage, business model, industry sector, and long-term objectives. Investor alignment matters enormously because the wrong capital partners can create strategic conflicts, governance problems, unrealistic expectations, or operational pressure that damages long-term company performance.

Founders sometimes become overly focused on obtaining capital quickly without evaluating whether investors truly support the company's strategic vision. However, institutional capital relationships often influence governance structures, board composition, operational priorities, and long-term decision-making for many years. Choosing investors carefully can significantly impact company culture, strategic flexibility, and eventual public market readiness.

One of the first things institutional investors evaluate before investing privately is whether the company demonstrates signs of future public market viability. Investors want to know whether the business possesses characteristics that may eventually support strong exit opportunities, acquisitions, secondary transactions, or IPO potential. This means companies must begin developing public-company-quality operations much earlier than many founders realize.

Operational maturity becomes increasingly important as funding rounds grow larger. Early-stage investors may tolerate operational imperfections in exchange for disruptive growth potential. Later-stage institutional investors, however, generally expect more discipline, stronger reporting systems, scalable infrastructure, governance oversight, and financial transparency. This progression reflects increasing investor expectations as companies mature. Businesses approaching institutional growth funding must demonstrate not only innovation and market potential, but also execution consistency, operational visibility, and leadership sophistication. Investors want evidence that the company can handle larger scale without collapsing operationally.

Institutional investors also evaluate the predictability of company performance carefully. Companies generating stable recurring revenue, improving customer retention, operational consistency, and reliable forecasting often appear more attractive than businesses dependent on unpredictable one-time transactions or unstable revenue streams.

Predictability reduces perceived risk. Investors prefer businesses where future performance can be modeled with reasonable confidence because this improves valuation visibility and long-term investment planning. Subscription businesses, recurring revenue platforms, infrastructure services, enterprise software, and highly retained customer ecosystems frequently attract institutional interest partly because they create more stable long-term revenue expectations.

Another major factor investors analyze is unit economics. Unit economics measure the profitability and scalability of individual customer relationships or operational transactions.

Institutional investors want to know whether customer acquisition costs, retention rates, gross margins, and operational efficiency support sustainable long-term growth.

Rapid growth without sustainable economics often creates concern because investors worry the business model may eventually collapse under scaling pressure. Companies capable of demonstrating improving unit economics as they grow generally attract stronger institutional support because scalability appears more financially durable.

Market leadership potential also strongly influences institutional investment decisions. Investors seek companies capable of becoming dominant players within expanding industries. Businesses positioned as category leaders or emerging market leaders often receive premium valuations because investors anticipate future market share consolidation and competitive advantages.

This is why investor-ready companies frequently focus heavily on positioning, branding, product differentiation, customer loyalty, and scalable infrastructure before public markets. Institutional investors understand that companies with strong competitive positioning often maintain pricing power, operational leverage, and long-term profitability advantages. Institutional investors additionally analyze management behavior carefully during fundraising processes. Investors evaluate whether founders communicate transparently, respond thoughtfully to difficult questions, handle pressure professionally, and demonstrate strategic discipline. Fundraising itself often becomes a test of leadership maturity.

Sophisticated investors can usually identify when founders exaggerate projections, avoid discussing risks, or prioritize storytelling over operational reality. Strong investor relationships are built on credibility, not hype. Institutional investors generally prefer realistic leadership teams capable of balancing ambition with disciplined execution.

One major mistake founders often make during fundraising is assuming investors only care about upside potential. In reality, institutional investors spend enormous amounts of time evaluating downside protection and operational risk. They ask difficult questions because they want to understand what could go wrong and whether management teams can navigate adversity effectively.

Investors evaluate customer concentration risk, regulatory exposure, technological disruption, leadership dependency, operational scalability, competitive threats, legal liabilities, cybersecurity vulnerabilities, economic sensitivity, and financial resilience carefully. Companies capable of addressing these concerns intelligently often strengthen investor confidence significantly.

Governance quality becomes increasingly important during later-stage institutional funding rounds. Investors frequently expect board oversight, financial controls, reporting standards, compliance infrastructure, and shareholder protections to mature alongside company growth. Weak governance structures can discourage institutional participation because they increase perceived operational risk.

Board composition itself often changes substantially during institutional fundraising stages. Experienced investors may request independent directors, audit committees, compensation oversight, and stronger governance frameworks designed to prepare the company for future public market obligations.

Institutional investors also place significant emphasis on capital efficiency. Companies capable of generating strong growth while using capital responsibly often appear more investable than businesses burning excessive cash inefficiently. Investors evaluate whether management deploys resources strategically and whether growth investments generate measurable operational returns. This does not necessarily mean companies must become profitable immediately. Many high-growth businesses operate at temporary losses while scaling aggressively. However, institutional investors still expect leadership teams to understand profitability pathways clearly and allocate capital intelligently rather than pursuing reckless expansion.

Another critical component of attracting institutional capital involves relationship building. Many founders incorrectly assume fundraising begins only when capital is needed. In reality, sophisticated fundraising often begins years earlier through relationship development, industry networking, investor communication, and reputation building.

Institutional investors prefer familiarity and trust. Companies that establish relationships with investors before actively raising capital often improve fundraising outcomes because investors gain time to evaluate leadership quality, operational consistency, and strategic progress gradually.

Regular investor updates, conference participation, industry visibility, thought leadership, and strategic introductions all contribute to long-term institutional relationship development. Investor-ready companies often build networks deliberately long before initiating formal fundraising processes.

Market timing also plays a major role in institutional fundraising success. Investor appetite fluctuates depending on macroeconomic conditions, interest rates, market sentiment, industry cycles, and public market performance. Companies seeking institutional capital during favorable market environments often achieve higher valuations and stronger investor participation.

However, investor-ready businesses focus more on operational readiness than purely external timing. Companies with strong fundamentals, disciplined execution, and scalable systems generally attract institutional interest across varying market conditions more consistently than businesses dependent entirely on temporary hype cycles.

Another important aspect of institutional fundraising involves signaling effects. When respected institutional investors support a company, additional investors often become more interested automatically. This phenomenon occurs because institutional participation itself signals credibility and reduces perceived uncertainty.

This signaling effect explains why certain companies experience rapidly accelerating investor demand once major institutional firms participate in funding rounds. Investor confidence becomes partially self-reinforcing as respected market participants validate the company publicly. Yet institutional capital also creates increased expectations. Once sophisticated investors participate, pressure for operational execution, governance discipline, financial reporting quality, and strategic growth often intensifies significantly. Founders must therefore prepare organizationally for the increased accountability institutional ownership creates.

Importantly, institutional fundraising should support long-term strategic objectives rather than short-term vanity metrics. Some founders become overly focused on maximizing valuation without considering dilution structures, investor alignment, governance implications, or long-term operational sustainability.

The strongest companies approach fundraising strategically. They raise capital to accelerate scalable opportunities, strengthen infrastructure, expand market positioning, improve technology, recruit talent, or prepare for future liquidity events. Institutional capital becomes a tool supporting disciplined growth rather than an end goal itself.

As companies approach IPO readiness, institutional relationships often become critically important. Existing institutional investors may support roadshows, introduce public market investors, strengthen valuation confidence, and provide credibility during the transition toward public ownership. Public markets frequently evaluate which private institutional investors supported companies before IPOs. Strong investor sponsorship can increase confidence significantly because public investors assume sophisticated private institutions performed substantial due diligence before investing.

Ultimately, attracting institutional capital before an IPO requires much more than simply presenting a compelling idea. Companies must demonstrate operational maturity, financial discipline, scalable infrastructure, leadership credibility, governance quality, strategic positioning, and long-term market potential.

The businesses that succeed in attracting institutional capital consistently are often the companies preparing for public market expectations years before officially entering public markets. They understand that institutional investors are not simply buying growth. They are investing in future public-company-quality enterprises capable of generating sustainable shareholder value over long periods of time.

The Startup That Earned Wall Street Before Going Public

When Rachel Kim founded her enterprise software company, she had no intention of becoming famous in financial markets.

Her goal was simple: build software that helped manufacturers reduce operational waste using predictive analytics and artificial intelligence.

In the beginning, almost nobody cared.

Manufacturing technology was not considered glamorous compared to consumer apps or social media startups. Venture capital firms frequently rejected Rachel's pitches because the industry appeared too slow-moving and operationally complex. Investors preferred trendy businesses promising explosive viral growth.

But Rachel understood something many investors initially missed.

Manufacturing inefficiency represented a massive global problem worth billions of dollars annually.

Her company's software helped factories predict equipment failures, reduce downtime, optimize inventory management, and improve operational productivity dramatically. Customers saved enormous amounts of money after implementing the platform.

The company grew steadily year after year.

Unlike many startups, Rachel focused heavily on operational discipline from the beginning. Financial reporting remained organized. Customer retention metrics were tracked carefully. Product implementation processes became standardized. The company avoided reckless spending despite pressure from some early investors to prioritize faster expansion.

Rachel believed long-term credibility mattered more than short-term hype.

For several years, however, institutional investors still showed only moderate interest.

The company generated strong revenue growth and profitability improvements, but it lacked the flashy media attention surrounding many venture-backed technology startups. Rachel occasionally questioned whether her disciplined approach was causing the company to be overlooked.

Everything changed during an industry conference in Chicago.

After speaking on a panel about industrial automation, Rachel met Daniel Whitmore, a managing partner at a major institutional growth equity firm. Unlike most investors Rachel previously encountered, Daniel asked detailed questions about operational metrics, customer retention rates, implementation scalability, and long-term margin expansion potential.

Rachel answered every question carefully with data and operational clarity.

Daniel became intrigued immediately.

Over the following months, his firm conducted extensive due diligence. Analysts interviewed customers, reviewed financial reporting systems, evaluated operational infrastructure, and studied management processes carefully.

What impressed them most was not just the software itself.

It was the maturity of the business.

The company operated with unusual discipline compared to many fast-growing private technology firms. Revenue forecasting proved highly accurate. Customer retention remained exceptionally strong. Unit economics improved consistently. Leadership communication appeared transparent and realistic.

Most importantly, the company looked capable of functioning successfully as a future public enterprise.

Daniel's firm eventually invested several hundred million dollars into the company at a valuation far higher than Rachel expected.

That investment changed market perception dramatically.

Suddenly, other institutional investors began paying attention aggressively. Analysts who previously ignored the business started publishing industry reports describing the company as a future leader in industrial AI infrastructure.

Additional funding offers arrived rapidly.

But Rachel remained selective.

She rejected several investors whose expectations conflicted with the company's long-term strategy. Some pushed for reckless expansion. Others wanted aggressive cost-cutting that could damage customer relationships. Rachel prioritized institutional alignment over maximizing short-term valuation.

Her disciplined approach strengthened investor confidence even further.

Over the next four years, the company expanded internationally, improved operational scalability, and deepened relationships with major enterprise customers.

Institutional investors consistently praised management execution and reporting transparency.

Unlike many startups chasing attention constantly, Rachel focused primarily on building operational credibility.

Then discussions about a possible IPO began.

Investment banks approached aggressively, believing the company represented one of the strongest enterprise software offerings preparing for public markets. Public market investors already recognized several institutional firms backing the company privately, which strengthened confidence immediately.

During IPO preparation meetings, one banker explained something important to Rachel.

"Public investors already trust this company before the roadshow even starts," he said. "Because the institutional investors supporting you have reputations for backing disciplined businesses."

Rachel realized the company had effectively earned credibility years before going public.

The IPO roadshow exceeded expectations.

Institutional investors responded enthusiastically because the company combined strong financial performance with operational maturity, scalable systems, disciplined leadership, and respected institutional sponsorship. Analysts described the company as "public-market ready" long before the IPO filing became official.

When the company finally listed publicly, demand surged. Shares opened significantly above the initial offering price. Financial media praised the business as one of the most operationally disciplined technology companies entering public markets in years.

After the IPO, a young entrepreneur asked Rachel what the secret to attracting institutional capital had been.

Rachel smiled before answering carefully.

"We stopped trying to look investable," she said. "And focused instead on becoming the type of company institutional investors genuinely trust."

That distinction changed everything.

Years later, the company became one of the most respected industrial technology businesses in public markets. Analysts praised management credibility, operational consistency, customer retention, and disciplined capital allocation repeatedly.

Rachel often reflected on how different her path had been compared to many startups chasing attention and inflated valuations recklessly.

Her company grew more slowly at first.

It received less media hype initially. But because the organization prioritized operational maturity, financial discipline, and long-term investor trust early, it eventually attracted stronger institutional relationships, better market positioning, and far more sustainable shareholder confidence.

And when public markets finally arrived, the company was truly prepared—not just financially, but operationally, strategically, and culturally—for the enormous responsibility of becoming a public enterprise.

Chapter 7

Preparing for the Scrutiny and Pressure of Public Markets

Taking a company public is often viewed as a major victory for founders, employees, and early investors. An initial public offering can create enormous wealth, unlock liquidity, increase brand recognition, and provide access to large pools of institutional capital. However, many entrepreneurs underestimate one of the most difficult realities of becoming a public company: life changes dramatically after the IPO.

Public markets create constant scrutiny, relentless pressure, and continuous evaluation. Once a company becomes publicly traded, leadership decisions, financial performance, operational execution, communication practices, governance standards, and strategic direction are examined by investors, analysts, regulators, journalists, competitors, and shareholders simultaneously. Companies no longer operate privately behind closed doors. They become public institutions expected to perform consistently under highly visible conditions.

This transition can be psychologically and operationally overwhelming for organizations unprepared for the realities of public ownership. Many businesses successfully complete

IPOs only to struggle afterward because leadership underestimated the demands of operating inside public markets. Investor enthusiasm during the offering phase may create excitement temporarily, but sustaining investor confidence over many years requires extraordinary discipline, adaptability, and operational maturity.

One of the most immediate changes companies experience after going public is the shift in accountability. Private companies primarily answer to founders, small investor groups, or limited stakeholders. Public companies answer to thousands or even millions of shareholders with varying expectations, investment time horizons, and risk tolerances. This complexity creates constant pressure on leadership teams to communicate clearly and deliver operational consistency.

Quarterly earnings expectations become one of the defining characteristics of public market life. Every three months, public companies must report financial results and explain operational performance to investors. Analysts compare actual results against forecasts carefully, and even small deviations from expectations can significantly impact stock prices.

Public market investors focus heavily on predictability because predictable companies are easier to value and model financially. Businesses that repeatedly miss projections or surprise investors negatively often experience declining credibility and increased stock volatility. This creates enormous pressure on leadership teams to balance operational ambition with realistic forecasting and disciplined execution.

Founders who previously operated with long-term entrepreneurial flexibility sometimes struggle adapting to the shorter reporting cycles and constant market reactions associated with public ownership. Private companies may tolerate experimentation, strategic pivots, or temporary operational setbacks quietly. Public markets, however, react visibly and often emotionally to uncertainty.

This does not mean public companies cannot innovate or take risks. Many of the world's most successful public companies continue evolving aggressively. However, public markets generally reward disciplined risk-taking supported by clear communication and measurable execution rather than chaotic unpredictability.

Investor relations become critically important after companies go public. Investor relations involves the ongoing management of communication between leadership teams and the investment community. Effective investor relations help shape market understanding, strengthen credibility, manage expectations, and maintain investor confidence during both strong and difficult periods.

Public company executives spend substantial amounts of time communicating with institutional investors, analysts, journalists, and shareholders. Earnings calls, investor conferences, annual meetings, interviews, and regulatory disclosures become routine responsibilities. Leadership teams must learn how to communicate strategically while maintaining transparency and regulatory compliance simultaneously.

Communication mistakes can create severe consequences in public markets. Poorly worded guidance, inconsistent messaging, unclear disclosures, or emotional executive behavior may trigger investor uncertainty quickly. Public markets react not only to financial results themselves, but also to how leadership communicates performance and future expectations.

This is why executive composure becomes extremely important. Public company leaders must remain disciplined during periods of volatility, criticism, competitive pressure, or operational adversity. Investors watch leadership behavior closely because communication style often influences market confidence as much as operational metrics themselves.

Media exposure also intensifies substantially after an IPO. Public companies attract attention from financial journalists, industry analysts, bloggers, competitors, activist investors, and social media commentators. Leadership decisions become public discussions. Strategic mistakes receive headlines. Operational setbacks may impact reputation immediately.

Founders unaccustomed to public visibility sometimes struggle emotionally with constant external criticism. Public markets can be psychologically exhausting because leadership teams operate under continuous observation. Investor-ready leaders must therefore develop emotional resilience and long-term strategic focus capable of withstanding temporary market noise.

Stock price volatility creates another major challenge. Public company valuations fluctuate constantly based on earnings results, market conditions, economic data, industry trends, geopolitical events, interest rates, analyst opinions, and investor sentiment. Even highly successful businesses may experience periods of sharp valuation swings unrelated to long-term operational fundamentals.

Many founders become emotionally attached to daily stock movements after IPOs. However, sophisticated public company leaders understand that long-term value creation matters far more than short-term volatility. Companies focused excessively on managing temporary stock price fluctuations often make poor strategic decisions damaging long-term shareholder value.

One danger public companies face is short-termism. Public market pressure can tempt leadership teams to prioritize quarterly results over sustainable long-term investments. Some companies reduce research spending, delay infrastructure improvements, avoid necessary restructuring, or manipulate guidance simply to satisfy short-term expectations temporarily.

While these strategies may occasionally support short-term stock prices, they often weaken long-term competitiveness eventually. Institutional investors increasingly prefer companies capable of balancing near-term operational discipline with long-term strategic investment. Leadership teams that communicate long-term vision clearly while executing consistently often build stronger shareholder trust over time.

Another major pressure public companies face involves regulatory compliance. Public companies must comply with extensive reporting obligations, securities regulations, governance standards, insider trading restrictions, audit requirements, and disclosure obligations. Regulatory failures can result in lawsuits, financial penalties, reputational damage, or shareholder litigation. Compliance infrastructure therefore becomes a central operational priority after public listing. Companies often expand legal departments, compliance teams, internal controls, audit procedures, and governance systems substantially to meet public company obligations effectively.

Cybersecurity risk also becomes more serious for public companies. Publicly traded businesses are attractive targets for cyberattacks because operational disruptions, data breaches, or ransomware incidents may impact shareholder value significantly. Investors increasingly evaluate cybersecurity preparedness as part of overall operational risk management.

Public companies must additionally manage shareholder expectations carefully. Different investor groups often possess conflicting priorities. Some shareholders prioritize aggressive growth, while others focus on profitability, dividends, operational efficiency, or long-term stability. Balancing these competing expectations requires strategic clarity and disciplined communication.

Activist investors may also emerge after companies go public. Activist investors purchase meaningful ownership stakes and attempt to influence company strategy, leadership decisions, capital allocation, governance practices, or operational restructuring. While activism can occasionally improve performance, it may also create strategic conflict and leadership pressure. Public market leadership therefore requires much greater political, strategic, and communication sophistication than many founders initially anticipate. Operating a public company involves managing not only operations and growth, but also investor psychology, market perception, regulatory relationships, media narratives, and shareholder dynamics simultaneously.

Employee morale and culture management become increasingly important as well. Public companies often experience internal cultural shifts after IPOs. Employees may become distracted by stock prices, liquidity opportunities, compensation changes, or increased organizational complexity. Leadership teams must work intentionally to preserve company culture while adapting to public market expectations.

Transparency inside the organization also becomes more important. Employees within public companies frequently monitor earnings reports, investor presentations, and external commentary closely. Leadership teams that communicate openly internally often maintain stronger employee trust and alignment during periods of market volatility or operational change.

Compensation structures also evolve after public listing. Equity compensation, stock options, restricted stock units, executive incentives, and shareholder alignment mechanisms become central elements of organizational management. Public companies must design compensation systems balancing employee motivation with shareholder expectations carefully.

Importantly, successful public companies develop long-term operational rhythms capable of supporting sustainable execution. They create forecasting systems, reporting processes, governance frameworks, communication protocols, and strategic planning cycles designed specifically for public market environments.

Many of the world's strongest public companies treat the IPO not as the finish line, but as the beginning of a new stage of organizational evolution. Going public provides access to capital and liquidity, but it also introduces entirely new responsibilities and performance expectations.

Founders who succeed in public markets often undergo major personal transformations themselves. The entrepreneurial mindset required to launch a startup differs significantly from the leadership discipline required to manage a public enterprise over many years. Public market leadership demands patience, emotional resilience, communication sophistication, strategic consistency, and operational discipline at much larger scales.

Companies that prepare properly for these realities often perform substantially better after IPOs because leadership enters public markets with realistic expectations rather than emotional excitement alone. They understand that sustaining investor confidence requires continuous execution long after the initial offering celebration ends.

Ultimately, public markets reward companies capable of combining transparency, operational excellence, strategic vision, financial discipline, leadership credibility, and long-term consistency. IPOs may create initial excitement, but enduring shareholder value is built through disciplined performance over many years.

The companies that thrive publicly are often those that prepared psychologically, operationally, financially, and strategically for the immense responsibilities of public ownership before ever ringing the opening bell.

The Founder Who Thought the IPO Was the Finish Line

When Jason Walker's cloud infrastructure company finally went public, he believed he had reached the summit of entrepreneurship.

The IPO generated enormous excitement across financial media. Institutional investors flooded the offering with demand. The company's valuation soared into the billions within hours of listing publicly. Employees celebrated life-changing stock option gains. Journalists praised Jason as one of the most successful technology founders of the decade.

For several weeks, everything felt surreal.

Jason appeared constantly on business television programs discussing the company's future growth plans. Analysts issued optimistic price targets. Investors praised the company's rapid expansion and strong recurring revenue model. Social media celebrated Jason's journey from struggling startup founder to billionaire CEO.

Privately, Jason felt relieved.

For nearly a decade, he had worked relentlessly building the company. Endless fundraising meetings, operational crises, hiring struggles, customer negotiations, and sleepless nights had consumed his life completely. The IPO felt like validation that all the sacrifices had finally paid off.

What Jason did not fully understand yet was that becoming a public company was not the end of pressure.

It was the beginning of an entirely different type of pressure.

Only three months after the IPO, the company prepared for its first quarterly earnings report as a public company. Jason assumed the quarter had gone well overall. Revenue growth remained strong, customers continued expanding usage, and new enterprise contracts were signed successfully. Internally, leadership felt optimistic.

However, Wall Street expected perfection.

During the earnings release, the company reported slightly lower customer expansion rates than analysts projected. Growth remained impressive by most standards, but investor expectations had become extraordinarily aggressive after the IPO excitement.

The stock dropped nearly twenty percent in one day.

Jason was shocked.

"How can this happen?" he asked angrily during an emergency leadership meeting. "We're still growing faster than almost everyone in the industry."

But public markets were no longer evaluating the company against private startup expectations.

Now the business was measured constantly against projections, analyst models, institutional expectations, and market sentiment.

The pressure intensified rapidly. Financial journalists criticized the company's slowing expansion metrics. Analysts questioned whether growth rates could remain sustainable long-term. Social media investors attacked leadership aggressively online. Employees became anxious watching stock prices fluctuate daily.

For the first time, Jason felt emotionally trapped by public markets.

Every public statement seemed capable of moving billions of dollars in valuation instantly. Every earnings report created massive anxiety. Every analyst question during conference calls felt loaded with pressure.

Jason began obsessively monitoring the stock price throughout the day. He slept poorly. He reacted emotionally to negative commentary. Leadership meetings became increasingly tense because Jason constantly worried about short-term market reactions.

The company itself remained fundamentally strong operationally, but leadership psychology was deteriorating.

One evening after another difficult analyst meeting, the company's chairman, Linda Mercer, requested a private conversation with Jason. Linda had previously led multiple public companies successfully over several decades. She understood the emotional shock many founders experience after IPOs.

"You're making a dangerous mistake," she told him calmly.

Jason looked exhausted.

"What mistake?" he asked quietly.

"You still think the market is judging your worth personally every day," Linda replied. "But public markets fluctuate constantly. Your responsibility is to build long-term enterprise value, not manage daily emotional reactions."

Jason remained silent.

Linda continued.

"Public company leadership requires emotional discipline. If you react emotionally to every market movement, eventually the company will start making emotional decisions too."

Those words stayed with Jason deeply.

Over the following year, he gradually transformed his leadership approach.

He stopped monitoring the stock price obsessively throughout the day. Leadership meetings refocused on long-term operational execution rather than short-term market reactions. Investor communication became calmer, clearer, and more disciplined.

Most importantly, Jason learned how to separate temporary market volatility from long-term business fundamentals.

The company continued investing heavily in infrastructure, customer retention, and product innovation even during periods when analysts pressured management for faster short-term profitability improvements. Jason communicated consistently that leadership prioritized long-term shareholder value rather than temporary stock fluctuations.

At first, some investors criticized the strategy.

But gradually, institutional confidence strengthened.

Operational performance remained consistent. Customer retention improved. Margins expanded steadily. The company executed predictably quarter after quarter without dramatic surprises or emotional leadership behavior.

Years later, the business became one of the most respected cloud infrastructure companies in public markets.

Analysts praised management discipline repeatedly. Institutional investors appreciated leadership transparency and long-term focus. Employees trusted company leadership because communication remained calm even during volatile periods.

Looking back, Jason realized the IPO itself had been psychologically misleading.

He originally viewed going public as the destination.

In reality, it was the beginning of a far more demanding leadership journey.

Private entrepreneurship required ambition, creativity, and resilience.

Public company leadership required emotional control, communication discipline, strategic patience, and the ability to withstand constant external pressure without losing long-term focus.

Jason eventually mentored younger founders preparing for IPOs. Many believed the public offering itself represented ultimate success.

Jason would smile thoughtfully before explaining the truth.

"An IPO gives you capital and visibility," he would say. "But staying successful as a public company requires an entirely different level of leadership discipline." Because in public markets, long-term trust is not built during the IPO celebration.

It is built quarter after quarter, year after year, through disciplined execution long after the opening bell stops ringing.

Chapter 8

Scaling Company Culture Without Destroying the Organization

One of the most overlooked yet critically important factors in building an investor-ready company is organizational culture. While investors often analyze financial statements, growth metrics, operational systems, and market positioning carefully, sophisticated institutional investors also recognize that culture influences nearly every aspect of long-term company performance. Culture affects hiring quality, employee retention, execution consistency, innovation, leadership development, operational discipline, customer experience, and organizational resilience during periods of stress or rapid growth.

As companies scale toward institutional funding and public markets, maintaining a strong culture becomes increasingly difficult. Many startups begin with passionate teams united around a shared mission, close communication, and entrepreneurial intensity. However, as businesses grow, complexity expands rapidly. New departments emerge, leadership layers develop, geographic expansion increases, communication becomes fragmented, and organizational identity often weakens. Companies that fail to manage culture intentionally during scaling phases frequently experience internal dysfunction that eventually damages execution quality and investor confidence.

Institutional investors understand this reality clearly. They know that operational systems alone do not guarantee long-term success. Businesses ultimately depend on people executing consistently across increasingly complex environments. Strong cultures create alignment, accountability, adaptability, and motivation that support sustainable scaling. Weak cultures often produce politics, confusion, turnover, inefficiency, and operational instability.

Culture can be defined as the collection of behaviors, values, expectations, communication patterns, and decision-making norms guiding how people operate inside an organization. It influences how employees solve problems, interact with customers, manage pressure, respond to setbacks, and align around company objectives. Unlike slogans or mission statements displayed on office walls, real culture is reflected through daily behavior patterns throughout the organization.

Many founders underestimate how quickly culture can deteriorate during rapid growth. Early-stage startups often operate informally because teams remain small and communication occurs naturally. Founders interact directly with employees, priorities remain clear, and organizational energy feels highly unified. However, once companies begin hiring aggressively, expanding departments, opening multiple offices, or scaling internationally, maintaining alignment becomes much more challenging.

One of the first cultural risks scaling companies face is communication breakdown. In small organizations, information flows quickly because employees work closely together. In larger organizations, information becomes fragmented between departments, management layers, and geographic regions. Misalignment increases. Priorities become unclear. Employees may begin operating according to inconsistent assumptions.

Investor-ready companies address this challenge proactively by developing strong communication systems and leadership structures. Regular operational meetings, clear organizational goals, transparent reporting, documented expectations, leadership accessibility, and internal alignment processes help preserve organizational clarity during scaling.

Leadership behavior itself plays a major role in shaping culture. Employees observe leadership actions far more closely than formal company messaging. If leadership teams communicate one set of values publicly while behaving differently internally, organizational trust weakens rapidly. Culture ultimately follows behavior, not branding.

This means founders and executives must model the standards they expect throughout the organization. If leadership prioritizes accountability, transparency, discipline, innovation, customer focus, or long-term thinking, those behaviors must appear consistently in executive decision-making and communication. Institutional investors often evaluate leadership culture carefully because leadership behavior eventually influences company-wide execution patterns.

Hiring quality also becomes increasingly important during periods of rapid scaling. Investor-ready companies recognize that every new hire influences organizational culture positively or negatively. Companies that hire aggressively without evaluating cultural alignment often create internal fragmentation over time.

Strong organizations develop disciplined hiring processes focused not only on technical qualifications, but also on communication skills, adaptability, accountability, and alignment with company values. Institutional investors frequently analyze employee turnover rates because high turnover often signals cultural instability, leadership dysfunction, or operational stress. Employee retention matters significantly because experienced employees preserve operational continuity, institutional knowledge, customer relationships, and execution consistency. High-turnover organizations frequently struggle operationally because constant employee replacement disrupts productivity and weakens internal cohesion.

One major challenge scaling companies face is preserving entrepreneurial energy while introducing operational discipline. Early-stage startups often succeed through creativity, speed, and flexibility. However, larger organizations require structure, systems, compliance processes, reporting standards, and operational controls to scale effectively. If companies introduce excessive bureaucracy too quickly, innovation and agility may decline. If they avoid structure entirely, operational chaos may emerge.

Investor-ready companies learn how to balance innovation with operational maturity. They preserve experimentation and creativity while implementing scalable systems capable of supporting larger organizations responsibly. This balance becomes especially important for companies preparing for institutional ownership or public market participation.

Accountability is another critical cultural characteristic institutional investors value highly. Strong accountability cultures create environments where employees take ownership of results, communicate problems early, and prioritize execution quality consistently. Weak accountability cultures often produce blame-shifting, inefficiency, political behavior, and declining operational performance.

Public markets reward consistency. Companies capable of executing reliably quarter after quarter often possess strong accountability systems internally. Employees understand expectations clearly, performance metrics remain measurable, and leadership addresses operational problems proactively rather than reactively.

Transparency also plays a major role in healthy organizational culture. Employees generally perform more effectively when they understand company goals, strategic direction, operational priorities, and performance expectations. Leadership teams that communicate openly often strengthen employee trust and alignment significantly.

This becomes especially important during periods of uncertainty, restructuring, or rapid growth. Employees naturally become anxious when organizations change quickly. Transparent communication reduces confusion and helps maintain morale during transitional periods. Institutional investors increasingly evaluate company culture because culture directly impacts long-term scalability. Organizations with strong cultures often outperform competitors over extended periods because employees execute more effectively, collaborate more efficiently, and adapt more successfully during market changes.

Innovation itself is heavily influenced by culture. Companies that encourage intelligent experimentation, open communication, and calculated risk-taking often generate stronger long-term product development and strategic adaptability. Fear-based cultures, on the other hand, frequently suppress creativity because employees become afraid to share ideas or challenge ineffective decisions.

Diversity of thought also contributes substantially to organizational strength. Investor-ready companies increasingly recognize that diverse leadership teams and employee perspectives improve problem-solving quality, innovation, market understanding, and strategic adaptability. Institutional investors increasingly evaluate diversity practices as part of broader governance and operational assessments.

Another major cultural challenge involves scaling leadership capability. Founders who successfully build small teams may struggle managing large organizations if they fail to evolve personally. Leadership requirements change dramatically as companies scale. Public-market-ready organizations require delegation, executive development, strategic planning, communication sophistication, and operational oversight capabilities far beyond early startup leadership.

Investor-ready companies therefore invest heavily in leadership development. Executive coaching, management training, succession planning, communication systems, and organizational design all become increasingly important as businesses mature.

Middle management quality also strongly influences culture. Employees interact with direct managers more frequently than executives, meaning middle managers significantly shape daily operational experiences. Poor management quality often creates morale problems, communication failures, and operational inconsistency even within otherwise strong companies.

Companies scaling successfully toward public markets typically prioritize management training and leadership consistency carefully. They understand that scalable culture requires scalable leadership throughout the organization, not just strong founders alone.

Remote work and distributed organizations have created additional cultural challenges in modern business environments. As companies expand geographically or adopt hybrid work structures, maintaining organizational alignment becomes more complex. Investor-ready companies increasingly invest in digital communication systems, collaboration infrastructure, virtual engagement strategies, and leadership visibility to preserve culture across distributed teams.

Culture also influences customer experience significantly. Employees operating within healthy organizational environments generally deliver stronger customer service, better product quality, and more consistent operational performance. Investors recognize that strong internal cultures often contribute directly to stronger external customer relationships and brand reputation.

Public companies face unique cultural pressures because stock prices, investor expectations, and public scrutiny may influence employee psychology substantially. Leadership teams must therefore work intentionally to maintain mission focus, operational discipline, and organizational stability despite external market volatility.

Importantly, culture compounds over time just like financial performance. Healthy cultures create positive reinforcement cycles where strong execution attracts better talent, stronger customer relationships improve morale, and operational consistency strengthens organizational confidence. Toxic cultures create destructive cycles producing turnover, confusion, declining performance, and reputational damage.

Some of the world's most respected public companies became successful partly because they developed exceptionally strong cultures supporting long-term execution. Employees within these organizations understand expectations clearly, trust leadership, collaborate effectively, and remain aligned around shared objectives.

Institutional investors increasingly view culture as a strategic asset rather than a soft secondary issue. Strong cultures reduce operational risk, improve scalability, strengthen retention, support innovation, and contribute directly to sustainable long-term shareholder value creation.

Ultimately, companies preparing for institutional investment and public markets must recognize that culture cannot be ignored while scaling. Growth amplifies organizational strengths and weaknesses simultaneously. Businesses that intentionally build healthy, accountable, adaptable cultures often scale far more successfully than organizations focused exclusively on financial growth alone.

Public markets may evaluate quarterly performance metrics, but long-term operational excellence is often rooted deeply within organizational culture. The strongest investor-ready companies understand this relationship clearly and invest accordingly in building cultures capable of sustaining growth, innovation, discipline, and resilience over many years.

The Startup That Almost Lost Its Soul

When Marcus Delgado launched his digital payments company, the culture felt electric.

The entire team fit inside a small warehouse office in Austin, Texas. Employees worked late voluntarily because they genuinely believed the company was building something important. Ideas moved quickly. Communication felt natural. Everyone knew each other personally. Problems were solved collaboratively without endless meetings or complicated approval systems.

Marcus loved the energy.

The company's mission focused on simplifying international payments for small businesses. Customers quickly embraced the platform because traditional banking systems remained expensive, slow, and inefficient for cross-border transactions.

Revenue growth accelerated rapidly as more businesses adopted the service globally.

Investors became interested almost immediately.

Funding rounds expanded aggressively. Hiring exploded. The company opened new offices in New York, London, Singapore, and São Paulo within only a few years. Employee count increased from twenty people to nearly three thousand.

From the outside, the company appeared wildly successful.

Internally, however, something dangerous was happening.

The culture was beginning to fracture.

New employees joined so quickly that onboarding became inconsistent. Departments developed conflicting priorities. Communication between offices weakened. Employees no longer understood company strategy clearly. Some managers focused heavily on internal politics and personal advancement rather than customer outcomes.

Marcus noticed subtle warning signs initially.

Customer complaints increased slightly. Employee turnover began rising. Meetings became slower and more bureaucratic. Departments blamed one another for operational problems.

Longtime employees quietly complained that the company no longer felt the same.

At first, Marcus dismissed these concerns.

"We're scaling," he would say. "Some growing pains are normal."

But the problems intensified rapidly.

One major product rollout failed badly because engineering and operations teams had not coordinated properly. Customer service became overwhelmed. Social media criticism spread. Several respected executives resigned unexpectedly within months.

More concerning, employee morale collapsed internally.

Many employees no longer trusted leadership communication because strategic priorities changed constantly. Some teams felt disconnected from company leadership entirely. Others believed executives cared more about valuation growth than operational quality or employee well-being.

Institutional investors began noticing operational inconsistency.

Although revenue growth remained strong, execution quality appeared weaker. Investors questioned rising turnover rates and declining customer satisfaction metrics during board meetings. Analysts privately worried the organization was scaling faster than its culture could support. Then came the crisis. An internal employee survey leaked publicly, revealing severe morale problems across multiple departments. Financial media outlets published stories describing toxic management behavior, communication breakdowns, and operational dysfunction inside the company.

The company's valuation suffered immediately.

Customers questioned whether operational quality was deteriorating. Investors pressured leadership aggressively for solutions. Employees became even more anxious watching negative headlines spread publicly.

Marcus felt devastated.

For years he had focused relentlessly on product growth, expansion, fundraising, and scaling infrastructure. He assumed culture would naturally take care of itself as long as the business succeeded financially.

He was wrong.

One evening after a difficult board meeting, Marcus sat alone inside the nearly empty headquarters office reviewing employee feedback reports. The company's chief people officer, Allison Greene, walked into the room quietly.

"You built a successful business," she told him carefully. "But somewhere along the way, we stopped building an organization people believe in emotionally."

Marcus remained silent.

Allison continued.

"Culture doesn't scale automatically. It has to be protected intentionally."

That conversation changed Marcus completely.

Over the following eighteen months, leadership focused intensely on rebuilding organizational culture from the ground up.

Communication systems improved dramatically. Leadership town halls became transparent and frequent. Management accountability standards strengthened. Hiring processes emphasized cultural alignment as heavily as technical ability.

Middle managers received leadership training. Employee feedback systems expanded. Internal collaboration improved across departments and international offices. Strategic priorities became clearer and more consistent.

Most importantly, Marcus changed personally as a leader.

Instead of focusing exclusively on growth metrics and investor expectations, he spent far more time listening to employees, improving organizational alignment, and reinforcing company mission consistently.

The transformation was difficult.

Some executives resisted increased accountability and eventually left. Certain operational restructurings created short-term disruption. Financial growth slowed temporarily while leadership stabilized internal operations.

But gradually, the organization recovered.

Employee retention improved significantly. Customer satisfaction increased. Internal communication became stronger. Operational execution stabilized across departments. Investors noticed the difference almost immediately.

One institutional investor later told Marcus something he never forgot.

"Strong companies don't only scale operations," the investor said. "They scale culture."

Years later, the company became one of the most respected digital payment platforms in public markets. Analysts praised operational consistency, employee retention, leadership discipline, and long-term execution quality repeatedly.

Marcus often reflected on how close the company came to losing its identity entirely during rapid scaling.

He realized culture was not a secondary issue separate from business performance.

Culture influenced everything.

How employees solved problems.

How leaders communicated.

How customers experienced the company.

How organizations adapted during pressure.

How businesses survived long-term growth successfully.

Marcus later mentored younger founders preparing for institutional funding and IPO ambitions. Many focused heavily on financial growth, valuation, and operational scaling strategies.

Marcus would always ask them one question first.

"What kind of organization are you becoming while you grow?"

Because he learned that companies capable of scaling culture successfully often became far stronger, more resilient, and more valuable over the long term than businesses focused only on revenue expansion alone.

Chapter 9

Strategic Growth, Expansion, and Building Long-Term Enterprise Value

One of the defining characteristics of investor-ready companies is their ability to pursue strategic growth intelligently rather than simply expanding aggressively without direction. Institutional investors understand that not all growth creates value. Some companies grow rapidly while destroying profitability, weakening operational discipline, exhausting employees, diluting shareholder value, or increasing long-term risk. Other companies scale carefully, strengthen competitive advantages, improve operational efficiency, and create durable enterprise value over time.

Public markets ultimately reward companies capable of generating sustainable long-term growth supported by disciplined execution and scalable economics. This means investor-ready organizations must learn how to balance expansion with operational maturity, innovation with discipline, and ambition with strategic focus.

Many entrepreneurs initially associate growth with revenue alone. However, institutional investors evaluate growth through a far broader lens. They analyze whether growth improves market positioning, strengthens margins, expands customer loyalty, increases scalability, reinforces competitive advantages, and enhances future cash flow potential. Growth that lacks strategic quality often creates operational fragility rather than long-term value.

Strategic growth begins with clarity regarding company identity and long-term positioning. Businesses that attempt to pursue every possible opportunity frequently lose focus, dilute operational execution, and confuse investors. Strong companies understand their core strengths clearly and expand in ways that reinforce those strengths over time.

Institutional investors frequently ask whether growth initiatives align with the company's long-term strategic direction. Does the expansion strengthen competitive positioning? Does it improve operational leverage? Does it increase customer lifetime value? Does it create defensible market advantages? Does it support future scalability?

Investor-ready companies approach growth systematically rather than emotionally. They prioritize opportunities capable of generating sustainable long-term returns rather than chasing short-term excitement or vanity metrics.

Market expansion often represents one of the most significant growth opportunities for scaling companies. Businesses may expand geographically, enter adjacent industries, launch complementary products, or target new customer segments. However, institutional investors evaluate whether companies possess the operational infrastructure, leadership depth, financial discipline, and strategic planning necessary to manage expansion successfully.

Rapid geographic expansion, for example, may create substantial opportunity while simultaneously introducing operational complexity, cultural challenges, regulatory risk, logistical difficulties, and execution pressure. Companies that expand too quickly without scalable systems often weaken operational quality and investor confidence.

This is why disciplined scaling matters enormously. Investor-ready companies often expand in phases, testing operational models carefully before accelerating growth aggressively. They analyze customer behavior, operational performance, hiring quality, market dynamics, and financial efficiency continuously throughout expansion processes.

Customer acquisition strategy becomes increasingly important during growth phases. Institutional investors examine whether companies acquire customers efficiently and sustainably. Businesses dependent on excessively expensive marketing or unstable lead-generation methods may struggle to maintain profitability long-term.

Strong companies develop scalable customer acquisition systems supported by branding, referrals, operational quality, recurring value delivery, strategic partnerships, network effects, or distribution advantages. Investors favor companies capable of growing customer bases while improving acquisition efficiency over time.

Retention rates also influence enterprise value significantly. Companies constantly replacing lost customers may appear operationally weak even if revenue grows temporarily. Strong retention demonstrates product-market fit, customer satisfaction, operational consistency, and long-term value creation potential.

This is why many institutional investors prioritize recurring revenue businesses so heavily. Recurring revenue models create predictability, improve forecasting accuracy, strengthen customer relationships, and often support stronger long-term margins. Subscription platforms, enterprise contracts, infrastructure services, and ecosystem-based businesses frequently attract premium valuations partly because retention creates durable growth foundations.

Product expansion strategies must also align with long-term operational capabilities. Some companies pursue excessive product diversification too early, creating operational confusion and weakening execution quality. Investor-ready businesses typically expand products strategically in ways that reinforce core competencies and strengthen customer ecosystems.

For example, software platforms may introduce complementary services increasing customer dependence on the ecosystem. Financial companies may expand adjacent products improving customer lifetime value. Healthcare companies may integrate additional services supporting patient retention and operational scale.

Institutional investors often reward ecosystem expansion strategies because ecosystem businesses become increasingly difficult for competitors to disrupt over time. Strong ecosystems improve customer loyalty, increase switching costs, and create operational leverage supporting long-term enterprise value.

Operational scalability remains critical throughout growth processes. Revenue growth unsupported by infrastructure often leads to declining service quality, employee burnout, customer dissatisfaction, and execution failures. Investor-ready companies strengthen operational systems continuously while expanding.

This includes technology infrastructure, leadership development, compliance systems, cybersecurity protections, reporting frameworks, hiring processes, training systems, and communication structures. Strong infrastructure allows businesses to scale efficiently without operational collapse.

Talent acquisition becomes one of the most important drivers of strategic growth as organizations mature. Institutional investors understand that leadership quality and employee capability strongly influence execution success. Companies unable to recruit and retain strong talent often struggle operationally regardless of market opportunity.

Investor-ready organizations therefore build employer brands strategically. They create cultures attracting skilled employees, leadership systems supporting development, and organizational structures capable of scaling talent effectively. Human capital becomes a major competitive advantage in modern capital markets.

Innovation also plays a central role in long-term enterprise value creation. Public markets reward companies capable of adapting continuously to changing technologies, customer behaviors, competitive pressures, and market conditions. Businesses relying entirely on current products without investing in future innovation often experience long-term stagnation. However, innovation must remain disciplined. Some companies pursue endless experimentation without operational focus or measurable returns. Investor-ready companies balance innovation with execution consistency carefully. They invest strategically in research, product development, automation, and operational improvement while maintaining financial discipline.

Acquisition strategy represents another important growth lever institutional investors evaluate carefully. Acquisitions may accelerate market expansion, strengthen competitive positioning, improve technology capabilities, or increase operational scale. However, acquisitions also create integration risk, cultural challenges, operational complexity, and financial exposure.

Poorly executed acquisitions often destroy shareholder value despite initial strategic excitement. Investor-ready companies approach acquisitions cautiously, focusing on strategic fit, operational integration capabilities, financial discipline, and long-term value creation rather than expansion for its own sake.

Capital allocation quality strongly influences long-term growth outcomes. Institutional investors evaluate how leadership deploys resources across hiring, technology, acquisitions, infrastructure, marketing, research, debt management, and shareholder returns. Strong capital allocation creates compounding enterprise value over time. Weak allocation often produces inefficiency and declining investor confidence.

One major challenge scaling companies face is balancing profitability with growth investment. Some businesses sacrifice all profitability indefinitely chasing expansion, while others become overly conservative and miss major market opportunities. Institutional investors generally prefer leadership teams capable of managing this balance intelligently based on industry dynamics and strategic positioning.

Public market investors increasingly value operational leverage. Operational leverage occurs when revenue grows faster than expenses, allowing margins to improve over time. Companies demonstrating strong operational leverage often achieve premium valuations because investors anticipate substantial future profitability expansion.

This is especially important during economic downturns or periods of market volatility. Businesses with strong operational efficiency and scalable cost structures often survive difficult environments far more effectively than organizations dependent on constant external funding or unsustainable expansion strategies.

Long-term enterprise value is ultimately created through consistent compounding. Investor-ready companies build systems, customer relationships, operational advantages, leadership depth, technology infrastructure, and market positioning gradually over many years. Sustainable value creation rarely occurs through isolated short-term events alone.

Public markets reward consistency because consistency reduces uncertainty. Companies capable of executing reliably across varying market environments often attract stronger institutional participation and maintain premium valuations over time.

Another important aspect of strategic growth involves adaptability. Industries evolve continuously due to technological disruption, regulation changes, economic shifts, consumer behavior changes, and competitive innovation. Companies unable to adapt strategically often lose relevance despite past success.

Investor-ready businesses therefore maintain long-term strategic flexibility while preserving operational focus. They monitor industry trends carefully, invest in future capabilities proactively, and remain willing to evolve business models when necessary.

Importantly, growth itself should strengthen the company rather than weaken it. Healthy scaling improves operational efficiency, leadership sophistication, customer relationships, brand positioning, and competitive advantages. Unhealthy scaling often creates complexity without strengthening long-term enterprise fundamentals.

This distinction explains why some rapidly growing companies collapse while others become dominant public enterprises generating enormous long-term shareholder wealth.

The strongest investor-ready companies understand that enterprise value depends not only on current revenue, but also on future durability, adaptability, profitability potential, market positioning, and operational resilience. Growth strategies must therefore support long-term strategic strength rather than temporary expansion alone.

Institutional investors ultimately allocate capital toward businesses they believe can continue compounding value over extended periods of time. Companies capable of combining disciplined growth, scalable operations, leadership maturity, innovation, and financial strength often become the long-term winners within public markets.

Strategic growth is therefore not simply about becoming larger. It is about becoming stronger, more scalable, more resilient, and more valuable with each stage of expansion. Companies that understand this principle position themselves far more effectively for institutional investment, successful public market participation, and enduring wealth creation over many years.

The Company That Grew Too Fast—and Then Learned to Scale Properly

When Nathan Cole founded his e-commerce logistics platform, investors praised his ambition constantly.

The company specialized in helping independent online retailers manage warehousing, inventory, packaging, and shipping through an integrated technology platform. Small businesses loved the service because it simplified operations dramatically while reducing fulfillment costs.

Demand exploded quickly.

Within three years, revenue increased more than tenfold. Venture capital firms competed aggressively to invest. Industry publications described the company as one of the fastest-growing logistics startups in the country.

Nathan became obsessed with scaling as quickly as possible.

New warehouses opened constantly. Hiring accelerated aggressively. International expansion began before domestic operations fully stabilized. Marketing spending increased massively. Leadership announced ambitious growth targets publicly during investor meetings. At first, investors celebrated the aggressive expansion.

Valuation estimates climbed rapidly. Employees felt energized by the momentum. Nathan appeared regularly on entrepreneurship podcasts discussing the future dominance of the company's logistics network.

But internally, cracks were forming.

Operational systems struggled to keep pace with expansion. Warehouses opened faster than management teams could oversee properly. Employee training became inconsistent. Customer support response times slowed. Inventory errors increased.

Some executives privately warned Nathan that the company was scaling faster than its infrastructure could support.

Nathan dismissed the concerns repeatedly.

"If we slow down," he insisted, "competitors will take the market."

Growth became the company's only priority.

Then the holiday season arrived.

Order volume surged beyond operational capacity. Warehouses became overwhelmed. Packages shipped late. Inventory tracking systems malfunctioned under pressure. Customer complaints exploded across social media.

Several major retail customers canceled contracts within weeks.

The company suddenly faced a crisis.

Investors became alarmed. Financial losses increased rapidly. Operational inefficiencies expanded across multiple departments simultaneously. Employee morale deteriorated because teams worked continuously in emergency mode.

For the first time, Nathan realized growth alone did not guarantee long-term enterprise value.

One particularly difficult board meeting changed his perspective permanently.

The company's lead institutional investor, Karen Whitfield, reviewed operational reports quietly before speaking.

"You built expansion," she told Nathan calmly. "But you didn't build scalable growth."

Nathan looked frustrated.

"What's the difference?" he asked.

Karen leaned forward slightly.

"Real scaling strengthens the organization as it grows," she explained. "Right now, every layer of growth is making the company weaker operationally."

Those words hit Nathan hard.

Over the following months, he began reevaluating the company completely.

Instead of opening new facilities aggressively, leadership focused on stabilizing existing operations. Warehouse management systems were upgraded. Employee training programs became standardized. Hiring slowed temporarily while operational accountability improved.

Customer service infrastructure expanded dramatically. Data analytics systems improved visibility into inventory performance, shipping delays, and operational bottlenecks. Leadership teams focused intensely on retention and execution quality rather than simply chasing revenue growth.

Initially, investors reacted cautiously because growth slowed substantially.

Some critics questioned whether the company had lost momentum. Media attention decreased. Competitors continued announcing aggressive expansion plans publicly. But internally, the organization became stronger.

Customer retention improved. Operational efficiency increased. Employee turnover declined. Profit margins stabilized. Most importantly, leadership finally understood how to scale infrastructure alongside revenue.

Nathan himself changed as a leader.

Previously, he believed success meant becoming larger as quickly as possible. Now he understood that strategic growth required operational discipline, scalability, and long-term value creation.

The company resumed expansion gradually over the next several years.

This time, growth looked very different.

New warehouses opened only after operational systems proved scalable. International markets expanded strategically rather than emotionally. Customer acquisition focused heavily on profitability and retention quality rather than pure volume.

Institutional investors noticed the transformation immediately.

One analyst later described the company as "operationally mature" rather than simply "high growth." That distinction significantly improved investor confidence.

Eventually, the company prepared for an IPO.

During roadshow meetings, institutional investors asked detailed questions about operational leverage, scalability, customer retention, and long-term margin expansion. Nathan answered calmly and confidently because the organization now possessed real operational depth rather than superficial expansion metrics alone.

The IPO succeeded successfully.

Years later, the company became one of the most respected logistics infrastructure businesses in public markets. Analysts praised operational discipline, scalable systems, leadership maturity, and strategic execution consistency repeatedly.

Nathan often reflected on how close the company came to collapsing under its own growth.

He realized the problem had never been ambition itself.

The problem was confusing rapid expansion with sustainable scaling.

True strategic growth strengthened the organization operationally, financially, culturally, and structurally with every stage of expansion.

And once the company learned that lesson, growth stopped becoming dangerous. Instead, it became compounding long-term enterprise value.

Chapter 10

The Long-Term Wealth Blueprint After Building an Investor-Ready Company

Building an investor-ready company is not simply about raising capital, increasing valuation, or completing an IPO. At its highest level, the process is about creating long-term wealth through ownership, strategic positioning, scalability, and disciplined enterprise building. Public markets, institutional capital, and equity events can create extraordinary financial outcomes for founders, executives, employees, and early investors—but only when organizations are built with long-term value creation in mind.

Many entrepreneurs focus intensely on short-term milestones such as revenue growth, fundraising rounds, or liquidity events while failing to think strategically about long-term wealth architecture. Yet the most successful founders in modern business history often built wealth not through isolated transactions, but through decades of disciplined ownership, strategic scaling, capital allocation, and enterprise value expansion.

Institutional investors understand this principle clearly. Public markets ultimately reward businesses capable of compounding value over long periods of time. Companies that maintain operational discipline, adapt strategically, allocate capital intelligently, and strengthen competitive advantages consistently often create far greater long-term wealth than organizations focused only on temporary hype cycles or short-term valuation spikes.

One of the most important concepts founders must understand is the power of equity ownership. Equity represents participation in future enterprise value creation. While salary and cash compensation provide short-term income, equity creates the possibility of exponential wealth expansion if the company scales successfully over time.

This is why institutional investors care so deeply about long-term scalability, recurring revenue, operational leverage, and durable competitive advantages. Businesses capable of compounding revenue, profitability, and market dominance over many years often create enormous equity appreciation for shareholders.

Founders who maintain meaningful ownership stakes during scaling phases may ultimately generate far greater wealth than executives focused primarily on short-term cash extraction. However, preserving equity value requires strategic discipline. Excessive dilution, poorly structured financing rounds, reckless spending, or weak governance can significantly reduce long-term shareholder outcomes even within growing companies.

This is why investor-ready companies approach fundraising carefully. Capital should accelerate sustainable enterprise value creation rather than simply supporting uncontrolled expansion. Every financing decision impacts future ownership structure, governance dynamics, strategic flexibility, and long-term wealth outcomes.

Institutional investors often analyze whether founders think like long-term owners or short-term operators. Founders focused entirely on immediate valuation increases sometimes make decisions damaging future enterprise durability. In contrast, leadership teams prioritizing sustainable scalability, customer loyalty, operational discipline, and strategic positioning often create stronger long-term shareholder value.

One of the most powerful wealth-building mechanisms in public markets is compounding. Compounding occurs when businesses continuously reinvest profits, improve operations, expand market share, strengthen competitive advantages, and increase operational efficiency over long periods. Small improvements repeated consistently can eventually create extraordinary enterprise value. Many of the world's largest public companies generated massive shareholder wealth not through explosive short-term growth alone, but through decades of disciplined execution and reinvestment. Institutional investors constantly search for businesses capable of sustaining compounding dynamics because long-term consistency often produces extraordinary returns over time.

Public companies capable of maintaining recurring revenue growth, operational leverage, strong customer retention, and disciplined capital allocation often experience increasing investor confidence and valuation expansion simultaneously. This creates powerful wealth creation cycles benefiting shareholders substantially.

Another important aspect of long-term wealth creation involves liquidity strategy. Liquidity refers to the ability to convert ownership into usable capital through stock sales, secondary transactions, acquisitions, dividends, or other financial events. Founders preparing for IPOs must think carefully about how and when to access liquidity without damaging long-term enterprise value or investor confidence.

Many entrepreneurs make the mistake of viewing liquidity events as opportunities for immediate lifestyle expansion rather than strategic financial planning. While successful exits can certainly create personal freedom, the most sophisticated founders often manage liquidity carefully to preserve long-term wealth growth potential.

Institutional investors generally prefer founders who remain meaningfully aligned with long-term shareholder interests after public listings. Excessive insider selling immediately following IPOs may create concerns regarding leadership confidence and long-term commitment.

This is why many successful founders structure liquidity gradually over time while maintaining significant ownership exposure to future enterprise appreciation. Strategic liquidity planning balances personal diversification needs with long-term shareholder alignment.

Tax planning also becomes critically important once equity value increases substantially. Public company founders often face complex tax obligations related to stock sales, options exercises, restricted stock units, capital gains, and liquidity events. Poor tax planning can destroy enormous amounts of wealth unnecessarily.

Investor-ready executives therefore frequently work closely with tax advisors, estate planners, attorneys, and financial professionals long before major liquidity events occur. Sophisticated wealth planning may involve trusts, charitable strategies, geographic planning, diversification structures, or long-term capital preservation approaches designed to protect wealth efficiently.

Another important long-term wealth concept involves capital allocation after liquidity events. Many founders achieve financial success through IPOs or acquisitions but later lose substantial wealth through poor investment decisions, emotional spending, or lack of strategic financial management.

Building wealth and preserving wealth require different skill sets.

Entrepreneurship rewards risk-taking, aggressive growth, and operational intensity. Long-term wealth management often requires diversification, discipline, patience, tax efficiency, and strategic asset allocation. Founders transitioning from private company building into significant personal wealth must therefore evolve financially as well.

Public company founders also face psychological transitions after major liquidity events. Many entrepreneurs spend years pursuing financial milestones believing wealth itself will create fulfillment automatically. However, long-term satisfaction often depends more on purpose, leadership legacy, strategic impact, and continued growth than financial outcomes alone.

Some founders lose direction after major exits because their identities become overly connected to the entrepreneurial struggle itself. Investor-ready leadership therefore includes personal development and long-term life planning alongside operational scaling and financial success.

Legacy building becomes increasingly important as wealth grows. Many successful founders eventually focus not only on personal wealth accumulation, but also on creating lasting impact through philanthropy, mentorship, investment activity, innovation, education, or future company building.

Institutional investors often respect founders who think generationally rather than transactionally. Companies led by long-term strategic thinkers frequently develop stronger cultures, healthier governance systems, and more sustainable growth models than organizations focused exclusively on short-term financial extraction.

Public markets also create opportunities beyond initial IPOs themselves. Companies with strong public market reputations may access secondary offerings, acquisitions, strategic partnerships, debt financing, or global expansion opportunities unavailable to private businesses. Strong market credibility becomes a strategic asset supporting future enterprise growth.

This is why maintaining investor trust after going public remains so important. Companies that preserve credibility, communicate transparently, and execute consistently often maintain stronger access to capital and strategic flexibility over many years.

Reputation itself becomes a form of long-term capital.

Founders known for operational discipline, ethical leadership, strategic execution, and shareholder alignment often attract stronger investors, employees, partnerships, and future opportunities repeatedly throughout their careers. Credibility compounds just like financial performance.

Another major long-term wealth factor involves ownership mindset. Investor-ready founders think differently about time horizons. Instead of focusing only on immediate revenue or valuation milestones, they focus on building durable enterprises capable of generating value over decades.

This perspective changes decision-making substantially.

Short-term thinkers often prioritize temporary metrics, media attention, or aggressive financial engineering. Long-term builders prioritize culture, customer relationships, operational quality, innovation, governance, and strategic resilience because they understand these factors support sustained enterprise value.

Public markets eventually reward durability. Companies capable of surviving economic cycles, technological disruption, competitive pressure, and leadership transitions often generate far greater cumulative wealth than organizations dependent entirely on temporary trends or unsustainable momentum.

This is why adaptability remains essential. Long-term enterprise value creation requires continuous evolution. Markets change. Technologies evolve. Customer expectations shift. Leadership teams must therefore maintain strategic flexibility while preserving operational discipline.

Investor-ready companies prepare continuously for future opportunities rather than reacting defensively after disruption occurs. They invest in innovation proactively, strengthen leadership pipelines, improve systems consistently, and maintain long-term strategic visibility.

Importantly, wealth itself should support freedom rather than dependence. Many founders initially pursue entrepreneurship seeking financial independence, only to become trapped later by external expectations, market pressures, or unsustainable lifestyles. Long-term wealth planning therefore includes intentional thinking about personal priorities, health, relationships, purpose, and life design.

The most successful founders often understand that money is ultimately a tool supporting larger goals rather than the final objective itself. Public markets may create wealth, but leadership legacy is often defined by what founders build, how they lead, and the lasting value they create for employees, customers, investors, and society over time.

Throughout this book, one central principle has remained clear: investor readiness is fundamentally about building trust. Trust in leadership. Trust in systems. Trust in scalability. Trust in governance. Trust in operational discipline. Trust in long-term execution.

The companies that earn this trust consistently often create extraordinary opportunities—not only financially, but strategically, culturally, and personally.

Institutional investors ultimately seek businesses capable of sustaining confidence through changing market environments. Founders who understand this principle build organizations differently. They focus not only on becoming larger, but on becoming stronger, more resilient, more scalable, and more durable over time.

And when those organizations eventually reach public markets, they often become platforms for long-term compounding wealth creation extending far beyond the IPO itself.

Because true enterprise value is not built during a single liquidity event. It is built through years of disciplined execution, strategic leadership, operational excellence, and long-term trust earned repeatedly over time.

The Billionaire Who Stayed Focused After the IPO

When Sophia Reynolds took her software company public, financial media described the IPO as one of the most successful technology offerings of the decade.

The company specialized in enterprise automation tools helping global corporations reduce operational inefficiencies using artificial intelligence. Revenue growth remained exceptional for years leading into the public offering, and institutional demand during the IPO exceeded expectations dramatically.

On the first trading day, Sophia officially became a billionaire.

Reporters surrounded her constantly. Business magazines featured her on their covers. Investors praised her leadership. Employees celebrated life-changing stock option gains.

Friends who once doubted her entrepreneurial ambitions suddenly viewed her as a financial genius.

For several weeks, the excitement felt overwhelming. Luxury brands offered partnerships. Wealth advisors flooded her inbox. Private investment opportunities appeared daily. Invitations to elite events arrived constantly.

Many people assumed Sophia would immediately begin living extravagantly.

But internally, Sophia remained surprisingly calm.

Years earlier, during the difficult startup phase, she had promised herself something important. She would never allow temporary financial success to distract her from long-term enterprise building.

Sophia understood something many newly wealthy founders failed to realize.

The IPO was not the final outcome.

It was simply a new phase of responsibility.

Only months after the public offering, market conditions became volatile. Interest rates increased sharply, technology valuations declined across public markets, and analysts began questioning whether software growth companies could maintain previous expansion rates.

Sophia's company stock dropped nearly forty percent within six months despite continued operational growth.

Financial media quickly changed tone. Journalists who previously celebrated the company began publishing skeptical articles. Some analysts criticized leadership for maintaining aggressive investment spending during uncertain economic conditions. Social media investors attacked management constantly.

Many executives inside the company became anxious.

Employees watched stock prices obsessively. Some investors pressured leadership to cut long-term innovation spending in order to improve short-term profitability metrics. Competitors reduced hiring aggressively and implemented layoffs.

The board asked Sophia whether the company should slow investment activity substantially.

Sophia listened carefully before answering.

"If we stop building for the future every time markets become nervous," she said calmly, "we'll eventually destroy the very advantages that created long-term value in the first place."

That decision defined the next decade of the company's future.

While competitors reduced innovation investment, Sophia's company continued strengthening product infrastructure, expanding internationally, improving automation systems, and deepening enterprise customer relationships.

The strategy created criticism initially. Quarterly earnings pressure intensified. Public market volatility continued. Some investors remained impatient.

But internally, the business grew stronger.

Customer retention improved. Operational efficiency expanded. Product capabilities advanced rapidly. Strategic acquisitions strengthened the company's ecosystem. Leadership continued allocating capital carefully toward long-term value creation rather than reacting emotionally to temporary market sentiment.

Sophia herself also approached personal wealth differently than many founders expected.

Rather than aggressively liquidating shares or pursuing extravagant consumption, she diversified gradually while maintaining significant ownership alignment with the company's future growth. She worked closely with advisors on long-term tax planning, philanthropy structures, and capital preservation strategies.

Most importantly, she remained emotionally grounded.

Sophia understood that wealth itself did not define success. Long-term impact, leadership integrity, organizational culture, and enterprise durability mattered more than temporary headlines or fluctuating stock prices. Over the following decade, the company became one of the most dominant enterprise software businesses in public markets.

The stock eventually multiplied many times beyond its IPO valuation. Institutional investors praised management discipline repeatedly. Analysts respected the company's consistency, innovation, and strategic patience.

Sophia's personal wealth expanded dramatically beyond even the original IPO success.

Yet she often reflected that the most important decisions happened after the IPO—not during it.

The company succeeded long-term because leadership resisted short-term emotional pressure and focused instead on compounding enterprise value patiently over many years.

At a leadership conference years later, a young entrepreneur asked Sophia what the biggest misconception about IPO wealth was.

Sophia smiled thoughtfully before answering.

"People think the goal is becoming rich," she said quietly. "But real wealth comes from building something durable enough to keep creating value long after the IPO excitement disappears."

The room became silent. Sophia continued.

"Anyone can chase a liquidity event. The real challenge is building an organization capable of sustaining trust, execution, and growth for decades."

That philosophy ultimately defined her legacy far more than the IPO valuation itself.

Because public markets may create wealth quickly.

But long-term enterprise building creates lasting value that continues compounding for generations.

At a leadership conference years later, a young entrepreneur asked Sophia what the biggest misconception about IPO wealth was.

Sophia smiled thoughtfully before answering.

"People think the goal is becoming rich," she said quietly. "But real wealth comes from building something durable enough to keep creating value long after the IPO excitement disappears."

The room became silent. Sophia continued.

"Anyone can chase a liquidity event. The real challenge is building an organization capable of sustaining trust, execution, and growth for decades."

That philosophy ultimately defined her legacy far more than the IPO valuation itself.

Because public markets may create wealth quickly.

But long-term enterprise building creates lasting value that continues compounding for generations.

Final IPO Thoughts

Building a Company That Deserves Public Market Confidence

The journey toward building an investor-ready company is far more than a financial process. It is a transformation of leadership, operations, culture, governance, communication, strategic thinking, and organizational maturity. Throughout this book, one central idea has remained consistent: institutional investors and public markets do not simply reward growth alone. They reward businesses capable of sustaining trust, scalability, operational discipline, and long-term value creation over time.

Many entrepreneurs initially focus on raising money, increasing valuation, or reaching an IPO as quickly as possible. However, the companies that ultimately succeed in public markets are rarely the companies driven only by short-term financial milestones. Instead, they are organizations that spent years building operational foundations strong enough to support the immense responsibility of institutional ownership and public scrutiny.

An IPO is not magic. Going public does not automatically solve operational weaknesses, leadership problems, financial instability, cultural dysfunction, or strategic confusion. In fact, public markets often expose those weaknesses faster and more visibly than private environments ever could. This is why investor readiness matters so deeply. Companies that prepare carefully before entering public markets often create far stronger long-term outcomes than organizations that rush toward liquidity events without building durable foundations first.

Institutional investors think differently from most entrepreneurs. Founders often focus on innovation, product development, customer growth, and market opportunity. Investors certainly value those things, but they also evaluate something broader and deeper. They evaluate resilience. They evaluate predictability. They evaluate leadership credibility, operational consistency, governance discipline, scalability, financial transparency, and long-term strategic positioning.

Public markets ultimately reward confidence. Investors allocate capital toward businesses they believe can continue executing effectively over many years despite competition, economic cycles, technological disruption, and operational pressure. Every system, leadership decision, governance structure, financial process, hiring strategy, and communication practice contributes to that confidence.

This means building an investor-ready company requires founders to evolve personally alongside their organizations.

The mindset required to launch a startup often differs dramatically from the mindset required to lead a scalable enterprise under institutional ownership. Early-stage entrepreneurship rewards speed, improvisation, and relentless risk-taking. Public-market leadership demands emotional discipline, strategic patience, accountability, communication sophistication, and operational maturity.

Many founders struggle with this transition because success itself creates new complexity. Rapid growth introduces hiring challenges, operational scaling pressure, investor expectations, leadership demands, cultural risks, regulatory obligations, and organizational fragmentation. The systems that helped a company survive as a startup may become obstacles later if they fail to evolve.

This is why intentional organizational development becomes so important. Investor-ready companies do not emerge accidentally. They are built deliberately. Leadership teams invest heavily in operational systems, reporting infrastructure, governance practices, cybersecurity protections, compliance frameworks, talent development, investor communication, and scalable culture long before public markets demand them officially. One of the most important lessons throughout this book is that perception and operational reality are deeply connected. Investor narratives matter because public markets invest heavily in future expectations. However, narratives unsupported by operational substance eventually collapse. Sustainable valuation expansion occurs when strong storytelling aligns with measurable execution consistently over time.

Companies that command premium valuations generally possess several common characteristics. They communicate clear long-term visions. They operate within large and expanding markets. They demonstrate scalable economics and operational leverage. Leadership teams behave credibly and transparently. Financial reporting remains disciplined and reliable. Governance structures create accountability. Organizational cultures support execution and adaptability. Customers remain loyal. Operational systems support growth predictably.

Most importantly, these businesses reduce uncertainty for investors.

Uncertainty is one of the greatest enemies of valuation. When investors cannot understand operational performance, leadership behavior, financial reporting, strategic direction, or long-term scalability clearly, perceived risk increases. Higher perceived risk almost always reduces investor confidence and valuation support. This is why transparency matters so much in capital markets. Companies do not need to appear perfect. Investors understand that every business faces challenges, setbacks, and periods of volatility. What matters most is whether leadership communicates honestly, responds strategically, and maintains operational discipline during difficult periods.

Trust compounds over time in public markets just like financial performance does.

Companies that consistently communicate transparently, execute predictably, and allocate capital intelligently gradually build stronger institutional confidence. That confidence often becomes one of the most valuable assets a public company possesses because it improves access to capital, supports valuation stability, attracts stronger investors, and creates strategic flexibility.

Another important theme throughout this book has been scalability. Institutional investors care deeply about whether businesses can continue growing efficiently over time. Growth unsupported by infrastructure eventually creates operational instability. This is why scalable systems, leadership depth, financial controls, cultural alignment, and operational consistency matter so heavily. The strongest investor-ready companies understand that scaling successfully means strengthening the organization with each stage of growth rather than weakening it through complexity or chaos. Operational discipline is not the enemy of innovation. In reality, discipline often enables innovation to scale sustainably.

Culture also emerged repeatedly as a defining long-term advantage. Many founders underestimate culture because it feels less measurable than revenue growth or profitability. However, culture influences hiring quality, employee retention, communication, accountability, customer experience, adaptability, and operational execution continuously.

Public markets eventually notice cultural weakness because culture affects execution quality directly. Companies with toxic internal environments often experience rising turnover, declining morale, inconsistent execution, and reputational damage over time. On the other hand, organizations with strong cultures often outperform competitors because employees remain aligned, motivated, and operationally effective even during difficult periods.

Institutional investors increasingly recognize this relationship. They understand that sustainable long-term enterprise value depends not only on financial performance, but also on organizational health and leadership quality. Leadership itself remains one of the most important variables influencing public market success. Investors ultimately place enormous trust in executive teams responsible for allocating capital, managing operations, navigating crises, and communicating with shareholders. Credible leadership strengthens investor confidence dramatically, while weak leadership can destroy enterprise value rapidly.

This is why leadership maturity matters so much. Public-company executives must learn how to balance ambition with realism, growth with discipline, innovation with accountability, and long-term strategy with short-term execution pressures.

Founders preparing for institutional ownership should understand that going public changes the nature of leadership permanently. Public companies operate under constant visibility. Every earnings report, operational decision, executive comment, acquisition strategy, or guidance adjustment influences shareholder perception continuously.

The companies that succeed long-term are usually the organizations capable of maintaining strategic focus despite market volatility and external noise. They understand that stock prices fluctuate, media narratives change, and economic cycles evolve. Yet long-term enterprise value is built through consistent execution year after year. Another critical lesson is that institutional capital itself is not the ultimate goal. Capital is a tool. It can accelerate growth, strengthen infrastructure, improve technology, expand markets, recruit talent, and create strategic flexibility. However, poorly managed capital often destroys organizations through reckless expansion, operational dilution, or unsustainable expectations.

Investor-ready companies approach fundraising strategically rather than emotionally. They seek aligned investors capable of supporting long-term company objectives rather than simply maximizing short-term valuation metrics. Strong investor relationships often become long-term partnerships shaping governance, strategic direction, and operational maturity.

The IPO itself should also be viewed properly. Many entrepreneurs treat public offerings as finish lines. In reality, becoming a public company marks the beginning of an entirely new operational phase. Public markets introduce continuous accountability, quarterly reporting obligations, shareholder pressure, regulatory oversight, and heightened scrutiny.

Organizations that prepare psychologically and operationally for these realities often perform much better after public listing because leadership enters public markets with realistic expectations rather than emotional excitement alone.

Importantly, not every company needs to pursue an IPO. Many excellent businesses remain private successfully or achieve liquidity through acquisitions, mergers, strategic partnerships, or secondary transactions. However, the principles discussed throughout this book remain valuable regardless of whether a company ultimately lists publicly.

Operational discipline, financial transparency, scalable systems, strong culture, leadership credibility, governance quality, and strategic positioning improve nearly every business outcome. These characteristics strengthen profitability, resilience, adaptability, customer trust, employee retention, and long-term enterprise value even outside public markets.

The process of becoming investor-ready therefore creates benefits far beyond fundraising alone. It forces organizations to mature structurally and strategically. It encourages founders to think beyond survival toward sustainability and long-term value creation.

As capital markets continue evolving globally, the companies most likely to succeed will be those capable of combining innovation with operational excellence. Investors increasingly reward businesses demonstrating adaptability, resilience, technological sophistication, scalable economics, governance discipline, and leadership credibility simultaneously.

The future will continue creating extraordinary opportunities for companies capable of solving meaningful problems at scale. Technological transformation, artificial intelligence, automation, healthcare innovation, digital infrastructure, financial technology, renewable energy, logistics modernization, cybersecurity, and global connectivity will continue reshaping industries dramatically over the coming decades.

Yet regardless of industry or market trends, one truth will remain constant.

Public markets reward trust.

Trust in leadership.

Trust in operational systems.

Trust in financial transparency.

Trust in scalability.

Trust in governance.

Trust in long-term strategic execution.

Every chapter of this book has ultimately pointed back toward that idea. Investor readiness is not merely about looking impressive temporarily. It is about building a business that genuinely deserves institutional confidence. The founders who understand this principle often build organizations capable of creating extraordinary wealth—not only through IPOs, but through decades of disciplined value creation afterward.

Because in the end, the greatest companies are not remembered simply for going public.

They are remembered for what they built after they got there.

www.ingramcontent.com/pod-product-compliance
Lightning Source LLC
LaVergne TN
LVHW040518210926
848480LV00007BA/1507
9798256015336